A CULINARY HISTORY OF THE

NEBRASKA SAND HILLS

· ·

RECIPES & RECOLLECTIONS
from Prairie Kitchens

CHRISTIANNA REINHARDT

AMERICAN PALATE

Published by American Palate
A Division of The History Press
Charleston, SC 29403
www.historypress.net

Cover images courtesy of the author.

Internal images courtesy of author unless otherwise noted.

First published 2014

Manufactured in the United States

ISBN 978.1.62619.556.1

Library of Congress CIP data applied for.

To all the residents, past and present, of the Sand Hills of Nebraska.

There was nothing but land, not a country at all, but the material out of which countries are made.

—*Willa Cather,* My Antonia

CONTENTS

PREFACE

I began seriously writing this book in the middle of a Nebraska winter, from my desk in a cold and drafty building in Burwell on the eastern edge of the Sand Hills. This is a partially renovated Carnegie Library whose large, single-paned windows are original, making them almost one hundred years old. When the prairie winds blow from the north, subzero-degree air howls through cracks in the windowsills and the spaces between the panes. On days when the high outside hovers around zero, it will be fifty degrees upstairs. I sit here in a hat and jacket, covered in a blanket, with a hot water bottle on my lap and a space heater pretending to warm the air under the desk. Writing in these conditions, my hands often go numb. Recipe-testing yeasted breads is a delicate balance between maintaining a hospitable heat in an oven on its lowest setting and watching a starter "like a sleeping baby," checking in on it every few minutes to make sure it is breathing and not too warm or too cold.

Every time I am tempted to complain about the conditions in this historic building, I look at all the books, notes, recordings and handwritten letters on my desk. These recollections of descendants from pioneers in the Sand Hills remind me that they were making these exact recipes, only in sod houses with no running water or electricity and in the same brutal cold from which I have protection thanks to bricks, electricity and meager heat. This perspective on hardship solidified my awe when asking myself, "How did they do it?" And then, "How did they eat?" The answers are as varied as the people asked, and I hope this book can bring us a little closer to a common experience of the past.

PREFACE

Time is invaluable when attempting to record a history before it fades away. The single most motivating factor to finishing this book came from one of my subjects, Eldora Muirhead, ninety-three. In one of our last interviews before I began writing, she said, "Hurry up and finish your book so I can read it before I die!" I have never had a more important deadline to meet.

ACKNOWLEDGEMENTS

I could not have written this book without the help of the Garfield County Historical Society; the ladies at the Cherry County Historical Society; Tammy Hendrickson and the Custer County Historical Society; Mari Sandoz High Plains Heritage Center; Union Pacific Railroad Museum; Nebraska State Historical Society; Irene Nelson Walker; Tammy and Jerry Rowse; Stephanie Bixby Graham; Dean, Delores, Keith and Mark Colburn; Isla, Tom, Max and Debbie Emerton; Melvin Hyde; Keith and Maralee Udell; Rosie and Marvin Murphy; Bob and Karen Hudecek; Dorothy Satra; Eldora Muirhead and Avis Reddaway; the "old-timers" table at the Legion Club in Burwell and the servers who lovingly harass them; Tenise Jarecke, Tammy Schmaljohn and all of the wonderful ladies at the Sandstone Grill in Burwell; Fred and Judy Reinhardt; Sharla Miller; and my husband and benevolent copy editor, Nick Guettler.

To all of those who shared their stories by writing, calling and sitting with me, and to the thousands of women over the years who submitted their recipes to community, church and local cookbooks for compilation and printing, this book is partly written by you.

INTRODUCTION

No matter what time of year, it is always a hypnotic drive through the Sand Hills of Nebraska. Its gentle hills are sculpted by the wind into graceful curves that repeat for hundreds of miles. They feel and look like rolling waves and have a similar effect to being on water—spellbinding, comforting and almost soothing in their vastness. When you're in these hills, you become enveloped in their calming, wispy movements, sedated by the whooshing white noise of the wind through the grasses. Reaching the end of the Sand Hills is like reaching a shoreline—a return to a different reality that feels a little like hitting land after being at sea for days. Outside them, in the "real world," things seem more terse, grid-like and ordinary. The Sand Hills is hiding in plain sight in Nebraska, and those who are adventurous enough to detour off Interstate 80 and go north will discover this unique, friendly and hard-won part of the country for themselves.

Memory, by definition, is a faculty of our mind, fallible and subject to mood and circumstance. Memories surround themselves with a context to which hindsight adds its own revisions. Never is this truer than with the memory of food, perhaps the most malleable memory of all. Food memories must be placed in context, present or past. Things taste better or worse depending on our mood and the events surrounding us while we eat.

Our recollections of a place or point in time, whether good or bad, deeply influence our reminiscences of food. I spoke with many Sandhillers, almost all of whom were raised on food grown on the land their families owned, and every single one reminisced about days when food "tasted better." Many of the cookies grandma served to us as children contained ingredients we don't (or won't) use today, like lard or oleo. Yet we remember scarfing down treats like "heavenly hash," containing cans of syrupy-sweet pineapple topped with frozen nondairy whipped topping as though it was the best dessert in the world. Then, it was. And now, when you consider the story of how that recipe came into the home, the love with which it was served and the community and family who gathered around the table to eat it, sometimes it still is. Many of these recipes stand up against time, but those that do not are no less important in telling the stories of a place than the blue ribbon pies, the prize-winning watermelons and the other countless garden successes and failures of the Sand Hills of Nebraska.

This book is the culmination of months of research, studying every cookbook published about or relating to the Sand Hills that I could get my hands on. I scoured historical societies, public and private libraries, yard sales and private collections for stories and recipes. I chatted with neighbors, friends and strangers alike and befriended more than a few generous Sandhillers as they trusted me to gather their stories and place them in a timeline within the larger story of what people ate, when and why. The recipes included are all adaptations of original recipes, except where noted. In some cases, my adaptations account for some technological advances available to us now that didn't exist fifty or one hundred years ago. Using a digital kitchen thermometer to tell exactly when the fried chicken is done is a great example. But many of the methods within these recipes are also exactly the same. A few necessary adjustments take today's palates into account, like the Sand Hills Short Cakes, which are a little sweeter and lighter than their predecessors.

Over the span of three months, I drove more than three thousand miles, crisscrossing the Sand Hills in search of recipes, history and stories. And yet I still couldn't reach every town, library and historical society in this vast region. What follows are amalgams of written and oral histories that were told and retold to me, along with research to create a general sense of shared history in a modern-day reminiscence. To be sure, for every person I sat down with there are ten more I couldn't meet to hear their stories, but it is my belief that the people contained in this book accurately represent the range of the Sand Hills experience.

THE SAND HILLS OF NEBRASKA

Beyond simply rural, residents and astute visitors describe the Sand Hills of Nebraska as open, rolling hills that one can get lost in. The hills themselves are peacefully monochrome—tans in the winter and greens in the summer, punctuated most days by a vast blue sky. Depending on the time of year, the greens below and blues above merge to almost appear like an ocean view. And just like on the water, the wind has a profound effect on the landscape. The grasses move in different, mesmerizing patterns like waves according to how strong the winds are blowing. There is a natural, immense beauty in this place.

If you type Dean and Delores Colburn's address into Google maps, it is not able to interpret the coordinates. This is perhaps the best way to illustrate how remote the Sand Hills is to the rest of the world. Instead, you'll need to know the Colburns or know someone who knows them. They will tell you to turn off the highway between two mile markers about thirty miles south of Valentine onto a crushed clay road that serves as their driveway. The moment you leave the highway, you are on their ranch, and if you stay on the road for five miles, you will still be on their land. After two and a half miles, you will arrive at their home in the middle of their six-thousand-acre ranch.

They are almost forty miles from the nearest town of two hundred. There is minimal cellphone service, and they are the last on the line of electricity, so when it goes out, they're also the last ones to have it restored. They have two backup generators for these rare but isolating occasions for the house and outbuildings. Delores has lived in Cherry County almost all of her eighty years, so she knows the land well. It's in her blood. Her grandfather Max Wendler took out a homestead claim on this ranch, and today, she and her husband, Dean, eighty-three, still work the land, with the help of one of their sons, Keith, as well as his wife and their son, Mark.

The fact that Delores's grandfather Max Wendler arrived in the Sand Hills at all is remarkable. He came from Germany with "five good kids and a hundred dollars" in the early 1900s to claim land in this sparsely settled territory. The country in which he arrived was not even properly mapped, as its boundaries were still forming. The Kansas-Nebraska Act of 1841 was an early full-scale government recognition to give shape to the Great Plains. The United States of America was just sixty-five years old and expanding at a record pace. The act made the Nebraska territory an accessible place, at least in theory. It was part of the new country taking shape, and with its definition came an invitation to be settled by intrepid new Americans, seeking to fulfill this nation's destiny of westward expansion. Settlers came in trickles at first, starting with the most daring and adventuresome.

Up until this point, the Sand Hills had been called "irreclaimable," "austere" and "a great desert of drifting sand." These more than nineteen thousand square miles of Nebraska (and a small part of South Dakota) represent the largest sand dune in North America and one of the largest "grass-stabilized" regions in the world. For almost one hundred years, the region was labeled the "Great American Desert" on maps. Explorers and cartographers simply couldn't find a better description for the enormous, seemingly empty and inhospitable land.

The Sand Hills sits atop the Ogallala Aquifer, the country's largest underground water source, which feeds at least eight states their supply of water. The geology here makes the Sand Hills land act like a sponge and a filter for rainwater and snowmelt to replenish the aquifer. It is also a place where industrial chemicals, oil spills and anything else applied to the land, intentionally or otherwise, will seep into the region's source of clean water. Perhaps more than anything, Sandhillers are proud to call themselves stewards of their land. That large, delicate shallow groundwater source not only gives the Sand Hills its characteristic shape but also sustains life here. The water table is so high (as little as three feet beneath the Sand Hills surface in some areas) that water surfaces in shallow ponds and lakes across the terrain, giving hundreds of thousands of migrating birds and land animals a much-needed place of rest and hydration. In fact, the Sand Hills is home to more than three hundred native and migratory bird species every year.

Windmills used to irrigate the land are almost as common as cattle in the Sand Hills.

This was some of the most difficult terrain to settle in the Great Plains. The land can't be plowed or it will blow away. That hard-learned fact is also what makes the Sand Hills one of the most well-known cattle ranching areas in the world. For such an austere, unpredictable region, Nebraska beef is responsible for 41 percent of the entire nation's annual beef sales. It adds $12 billion to Nebraska's economy every year. So, growing grass is big business in small towns in the Sand Hills and all over the state.

Delores and Dean ranch in Cherry County, the largest county in the state. But most ranchers out here don't consider themselves cattle ranchers. "What we've got to sell is that grass," Delores says as she looks out her ranch house window. Dean and Delores still work their grass and the cattle that graze it every day, despite the fact that Delores describes herself and her husband as "retired."

In the Sand Hills today, a "modest" ranching operation is 4,000 to 6,000 acres. "Average" ranches are upward of 10,000 acres. By comparison, Central Park in New York City is 843 acres (1.3 square miles). Dean and Delores's modest ranch covers more than 9.0 square miles and can fit seven Central Parks inside it, with enough space left over for their family's houses, outbuildings and corrals. It's a long way to travel to borrow a cup of sugar for a recipe, and this immense scale is part of why ranch families have come to be so independent. It also helps explain why recipes in this area evolved the way they did.

The area is hot in the summer and cold in the winter. Temperatures can swing fifty degrees or more in one day; a spring morning can start out at twenty-five degrees and increase to seventy-five to eighty by midafternoon. It is an area prone to destructive rains, debilitating drought, snowstorms and hailstorms, as well as tornadoes. To survive, everyone must be a keen observer of nature in this agriculturally centered place. Delores has earned an honorary title in the nearest large town of Valentine, almost forty miles north, as the radio station's "Southern Bureau." She regularly calls in to report weather systems she observes developing in the southern part of the county.

Their ranch is about 400 feet higher in elevation than Valentine, which sits relatively high on the Great Plains at 2,590 feet above sea level. Her reports illustrate how different the weather can be in such a short distance and elevation. She calls in whenever the ranch receives remarkable rain, snow or hail or if it is exceptionally cold or hot. "People stop me when I go into town and say I must have quite the weather station on the ranch." She laughs. "My weather forecasting is a rain gauge and a yardstick." She's also a storm chaser for the North Platte station ninety miles south, although she confesses that the term is a bit misleading. "Anything between the back door and the rain gauge, I'll call it in."

Identifying a place as "rural" is a classification defined more by what it is not than by what it is. A rural area is *not* populated with more than 1,000 people per square mile. It does *not* have a city containing more than 50,000 people nearby. The Health Resources and Services Administration's Rural Services Department tries to clarify these definitions by saying, "Whatever is not urban is considered rural." The nearest major city is Omaha, population 425,000, from which the center of the Sand Hills is a six-hour drive. By contrast, the most interior county of the Sand Hills, Thomas County, held 676 people in its 714 square miles in 2012. Depending on the shifting sands (and definitions), the Sand Hills spread across twenty-five counties of Nebraska, all of which are considered rural.

The interior has never had a large town; the closest ones have always been at the edges and the result of nationwide expansion. North Platte is a railroad town on the southern edge and still holds 25,000 residents. At one point in time, as the railroads progressed building west, it was the terminus for the Union Pacific Railroad. When the railroad became transcontinental in 1869, it left North Platte with the largest rail classification yards in the world—still today holding that title. Even on this southern edge, this was a tremendously important lifeline to interior Sand Hills residents. Alliance, the next-largest town of 8,500, sits on the western edge, sprawling across cropland that comes to a startling halt where the signature rolling dunes of the Sand Hills start. Town sizes decrease significantly the farther into the Sand Hills one travels. In the middle swath of the Sand Hills, one can drive sixty miles in between towns, and each town contains fewer than 500 people.

This insulation from the outside world has preserved some of the last rural, small-town life left in the United States. Contained in this way of life is a set of skills required for self-sufficiency that makes a stoic Renaissance man or woman out of everyone. To continue this way of life, most ranchers, male or female, might know how to fix a mechanical engine, break a horse, fix a windmill, can fifty quarts of tomatoes, repair upholstery, plant and harvest a large garden, build a fence or building, garden and tend orchards and raise and butcher chickens—skills that are all but gone in most urban environments. It's out of necessity; oftentimes there simply isn't anyone to call to come fix something.

What some would consider drawbacks, others call assets. The very geography that isolates also shapes and unifies the people who live there today. If the grocery store closed tomorrow, Dean, Delores and family would survive. If the nearest town's mechanic closed up shop, one of their sons would step up the auto maintenance. All of these things can and do happen in the Sand Hills. It's part of what makes the area unique yet also presents a paradox. It is a land and a lifestyle both dying and thriving at the same time, but if you stop to pay attention, that's no different than Mother Nature itself.

The Sand Hills has a particular brand of helpful friendliness found in one of the last remaining cowboy lifestyles as well. On the sparsely traveled roads, you'll encounter "the wave"—usually two fingers lifted off a rugged hand at the top of a pickup truck's steering wheel. It's a friendly, connecting wave, welcoming everyone who passes by, because someone passing by is itself an occasion to be marked on these desolate highways. The Colburns and others like them are among the last of this way of life, part of a legacy that contains "real-life" cowboys—"simple" ranchers who suffer the stigma of rural hick folk projected by the ever-growing urban regions. What the stereotype doesn't account for is that in order to make it this far, beating the odds of Mother Nature against you, your grass, your crops and your livelihood, you must be among the most resilient and adaptable businessmen and businesswomen in the country.

Ranching is a way of life, but it's also serious business. To succeed, operations must maximize efficiencies on the ranch at home. Bets right back

Information for future reference, indeed. This pocket notebook from 1895 contains details of plantings on the Wendler ranch, with notations of what worked and what didn't, as well as new and experimental plantings. *Courtesy of Dean and Delores Colburn.*

at Mother Nature must be hedged and collaborations with other businesses that share a common goal formed—all so cattle can be sold at the best prices on the open market. Dean and Delores are great examples of the rugged individualism and do-it-yourself spirit of the people who tend these grasses. They are resourceful and adept at solving the many problems of ranch life. The only "simple" part of this way of life is the end goal: to tend the grass and remain independent for another year on land that has now seen five generations of family come and go.

On Delores's ranch one afternoon, we sat down to a dinner (the big noontime meal) of baked chicken and stuffing. The table was set with Dorothy Lynch dressing and a bottle of homemade vinegar from a vinegary in nearby Cody, Nebraska. We had a side of a sweet-sour apple and celery salad. For dessert, we ate lemon pie. This is a common ranch meal today, but it took the Colburns' ancestors more than one hundred years of working the land to get to a place where we could call this a typical meal. If you look closely, the food on every table here in the Sand Hills tells its own story about the region and its permanent settlers. Triumphs, experiments, hospitality, successes and failures, past homelands and current opportunities can all be seen by looking at what's for dinner on the kitchen table.

THE HOMESTEAD ACT

E xploratory missions to entice early Americans to inhabit the continent
were but trickles from behind the floodgates of settlement about to open
in the 1800s. In the middle of the Civil War, President Abraham Lincoln
watched eleven states leave the Union and the country battle for its own
life to survive the split. In the middle of wartime, he signed the Homestead
Act of 1862. Filled with political potential, the act was a way to expand
Union territory and strength. It was also a way for the new country to regain
some revenue by creating saleable land. It specifically allowed citizens, those
intending to become citizens and "anyone who never borne arms against the
U.S. Government" to acquire land. This was an effective blow against the
Confederacy, rewarding the Union and preventing the spread of separation
and the slavery that came with it.

Hundreds of years before American migrants and European immigrants
even had this new opportunity to succeed on free land, the middle continent
was explored by Spanish and French settlers. The Spanish explored territory
north of what is now Mexico, setting out from their posts in Santa Fe in
the 1500s. It would be two hundred years before the French would explore
the region in 1714, northward from what is now Louisiana, followed by
Merriwether Lewis and William Clark's famous American expedition in
1804. With the Louisiana Purchase in 1803, what is now called the Sand
Hills officially became United States land.

The intrepid American explorers began their exploration in Illinois and
traveled through northern Nebraska via the Missouri and Niobrara Rivers,

ending in Seaside, Oregon, in 1806. With their return from the West came word of rich, diverse lands filled with countless new varieties of flora and fauna, as well as the possibility of opening up the continent to trade with other continents, crucial for a burgeoning country's expansion. The impact on food history was not as remarkable. These expedition teams packed food necessary only for survival and foraged the rest. Expedition members lived off the land, which in the best of times included an abundance of fish as well as game such as buffalo, elk and deer. In the worst of times, rabbit and flour mixed with foraged berries.

Shortly after, other adventuresome migrants trickled west and "squatted" on land, allowing them to claim it and purchase it from the U.S. government at a discounted rate of $1.25 per acre. The California Gold Rush in 1849 brought a flood of fortune-seekers west (and sent many back whence they came). This first settlement flurry brought a trickle of people into the Great Plains and Nebraska, mostly to travel across it, but settlers, land speculators and cattle ranchers from territories south soon began claiming it for themselves.

When the Homestead Act became law, it allowed eligible citizens and citizen hopefuls to file a claim for 160 acres of unappropriated government land for free, though under one condition: you had to live on the land for five years, making improvements and demonstrating the ability to make a living from it. Nebraska was still crudely mapped territory and not yet a state in the Union, but in its infancy lies a particular distinction: it is home to one of the first "homesteaders" (as claimants would come to be called) to file for land under the act. On January 1, 1863, the first day the act went into effect, Daniel Freeman, a Union army scout, convinced a clerk at a New Year's Eve party to open the land office in Brownville, Nebraska, shortly after midnight and make his claim.

Land survey offices and the U.S. government took an approach to settling the new territory that relied on the global latitude and longitudinal lines to be able to map and divide territory in perfectly square sections of 640 acres each. Freeman filed his claim for 160 acres, a "quarter section" of the amount set forth as a "homestead plot" by the government. He paid $1.25 in registration fees and promised to improve the land for five years. (Freeman and other Civil War veterans and service members like him were allowed a special exception. He could deduct his length of service in the war from that time.)

Freeman and 416 others were the first people to claim homesteads the day the Homestead Act went into effect, and the race was on. Four years later, the state of Nebraska joined the Union. By the time the Homestead Act ended in 1976, more than 270 million acres of land had been claimed by 4 million claimants, more than 10 percent of what is now the United States. But underlying the veneer of success was a harsher reality: ultimately, less than half (about 1.6 million) of the claims would be successful. Today, part of Freeman's original homestead is now the site of the Homestead National Monument outside Beatrice, Nebraska.

About 150 years later, I'm sitting with Delores and Dean at their kitchen table on land claimed the same way. "Be careful with those dates, Dean." Delores turns to me and says, "He always gets us married a year after our daughter was born. They do that now, but they didn't then!" She laughs and jokes with Dean, "So get it right!" They were married in the fall of 1951, had their first daughter and moved onto her family's land in 1953. Each year, they raise hundreds of cattle on the grass that once was owned by Delores's grandfather Max and great uncle Gus Wendler. Great Uncle Gus came to America from Germany, and in 1883, he claimed a plot of land, like many others, through the Homestead Act.

The original house her grandfather had built for her grandmother and growing family in the late 1900s is still on the property, although it's used as an equipment storage shed now. Today, Dean and Delores live in the house built by her father on the property in the 1940s. Their son, Keith, and his wife, Kristi, also live on the ranch in a house they built just a quarter mile away. Keith and Kristi's son, Mark, has joined the family operation as well, living in his own house up the hill—a total of three generations actively working the land. They all help maintain every aspect of the ranch, from raising cattle and hogs to fixing windmills, cars and tractors. In all, five generations of their family have been on the land. Just like Grandfather Max and Great Uncle Gus, they are very lucky to have made it this far, and they are grateful for it every day.

The pre-1900s waves of homesteaders coming to Nebraska often found themselves competing with the land claims of cattlemen and ranchers already in the area, who often took the best lands for themselves and their cattle. The plains consisted of open, unfenced rangeland at this point, with established cattle drive trails extending north from Texas in search of forage for massive herds of cattle. The purpose of these months-long drives was to get the cattle to faraway railroad stops to transport them to markets and required the animals to forage what was available along the way. Drives pushed through newly claimed private lands, mixing up herds and decimating much-needed grass and newly planted crops. According to a common legend, the Sand Hills became cattle country accidentally when a storm disoriented a herd of cattle and scattered them into the region, where they were later discovered to be thriving on the grass.

Homesteaders started to draw figurative lines in the sand by erecting barbed wire fencing to try and keep outside cattle off their lands, but it would be thirty years after the Homestead Act that the U.S. government would step in to regulate the free ranging of cattle and uphold individual ranchers' rights to do so. In another challenge, the lure of free land brought fraudulent efforts to grab more than 160 acres. But all told, it represented such an opportunity that it created a significant American migration from the East, as well as European immigration. The act and the land promised a new start, property ownership and control of one's own destiny—a dream that proved irresistible to many.

Many settlers came westward by covered wagon, or bull train, which is pretty much as it sounds: a large wagon pulled by multiples of oxen, allowing

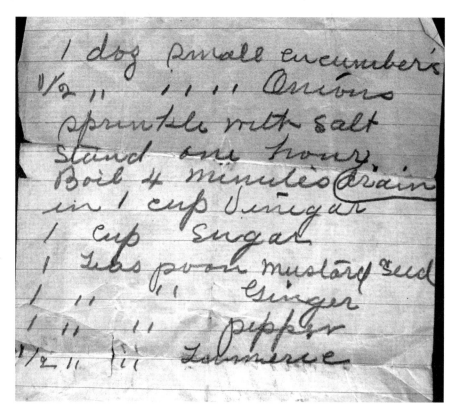

A handwritten recipe for quick pickles. Most early recipes exist in list form, without memorializing technique, times or temperatures. *Recipe archived at the Cherry County Historical Society Museum, Valentine, Nebraska.*

more families and goods to arrive at one time. Others came upriver on steamships and portaged across Nebraska. The town of Brownville was a very popular migrant landing point on the Missouri River, at one point taking on more than one hundred new settlers per day. After the railroads were built, settlers could arrive on "emigrant trains"—essentially boxcars fitted for passenger travel. Using rough maps and the government's reassurance that this was the country's destiny, families came with food, perhaps a cast-iron stove and the tools they thought they needed to build new lives.

The first foods on the wagons were simple: flour, lard, dried or smoked beef, clarified butter (the fat skimmed off so it wouldn't go bad), cornmeal, raw coffee beans, dried beans, bacon and salted pork. On occasion, there was also dried fruit, cans of vegetables, dried fish and beef, sugar, grease for cooking and spices like cinnamon, clove and nutmeg. Whiskey was brought for crude water and utensil purification purposes. Small batches of molasses were brought, but the heavy liquid was often rationed. "Hardtack" was a biscuit made from flour and water and baked into what would charitably be called a pellet; it was a reliable food source dipped in coffee to make it go down more easily. With this kind of pantry, there was not much use for cookbooks.

Many homesteaders arriving to make their claims for free Sand Hills land at government offices had never seen or heard details about the land before. There, they picked out land on a map and then arrived to learn that most of the land was not farmable. Those lucky enough to settle by rivers or have one of the Sand Hills' many precious lakes on their property might have had patches of more workable soil to plant gardens. The majority that settled on dry land hoped to find any low-lying patch of soil in the valleys of the sandy hills so they could try to make it workable for garden plants. Wives, upon seeing the new land, reportedly cried at the sight. Looking out across a landscape made entirely of sand, with only grass to hold it down, there was "nothing to cast a shadow" on the land. Trees are not native to the Sand Hills. Many early settlers slept in or under their wagons until the first shelters were built. Dugouts (modified caves excavated from the sides of hills) or sod houses (small square structures made of blocks of earth "busted" out of compacted ground with a plow and stacked like bricks to make walls) were these first structures.

When improvements to the land were able to be made, they came in the form of sod barns, stables and chicken houses. This came to be known as the "sod house era," or the first wave of settlement, roughly from the 1860s to the 1910s; during this time, most, if not all, settlers first built and lived in

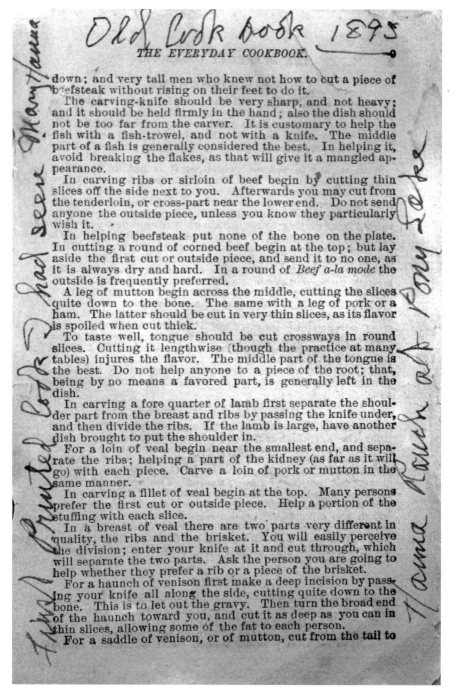

Old Cook book 1895

THE EVERYDAY COOKBOOK.

down; and very tall men who knew not how to cut a piece of beefsteak without rising on their feet to do it.

The carving-knife should be very sharp, and not heavy; and it should be held firmly in the hand; also the dish should not be too far from the carver. It is customary to help the fish with a fish-trowel, and not with a knife. The middle part of a fish is generally considered the best. In helping it, avoid breaking the flakes, as that will give it a mangled appearance.

In carving ribs or sirloin of beef begin by cutting thin slices off the side next to you. Afterwards you may cut from the tenderloin, or cross-part near the lower end. Do not send anyone the outside piece, unless you know they particularly wish it.

In helping beefsteak put none of the bone on the plate. In cutting a round of corned beef begin at the top; but lay aside the first cut or outside piece, and send it to no one, as it is always dry and hard. In a round of *Beef a-la mode* the outside is frequently preferred.

A leg of mutton begin across the middle, cutting the slices quite down to the bone. The same with a leg of pork or a ham. The latter should be cut in very thin slices, as its flavor is spoiled when cut thick.

To taste well, tongue should be cut crossways in round slices. Cutting it lengthwise (though the practice at many tables) injures the flavor. The middle part of the tongue is the best. Do not help anyone to a piece of the root; that, being by no means a favored part, is generally left in the dish.

In carving a fore quarter of lamb first separate the shoulder part from the breast and ribs by passing the knife under, and then divide the ribs. If the lamb is large, have another dish brought to put the shoulder in.

For a loin of veal begin near the smallest end, and separate the ribs; helping a part of the kidney (as far as it will go) with each piece. Carve a loin of pork or mutton in the same manner.

In carving a fillet of veal begin at the top. Many persons prefer the first cut or outside piece. Help a portion of the stuffing with each slice.

In a breast of veal there are two parts very different in quality, the ribs and the brisket. You will easily perceive the division; enter your knife at it and cut through, which will separate the two parts. Ask the person you are going to help whether they prefer a rib or a piece of the brisket.

For a haunch of venison first make a deep incision by passing your knife all along the side, cutting quite down to the bone. This is to let out the gravy. Then turn the broad end of the haunch toward you, and cut it as deep as you can in thin slices, allowing some of the fat to each person.

For a saddle of venison, or of mutton, cut from the tail to

Written on the pages: "The first printed book I had seen. Old cook book 1895." This is a section of *The Everyday Cookbook* by Miss E. Neil, originally published in 1892. *Book archived at the Cherry County Historical Society Museum, Valentine, Nebraska.*

such structures until other improvements could be made. If families physically and economically survived this period, wood-framed structures were later built on the same properties to replace the first structures. Roads, banks, general stores and post offices all needed to be built with materials shipped from the East. Trees needed to be planted for protection against brutal prairie winds and sun. These settlers had formidable obstacles to overcome, but the former

A sod house was usually the first improvement built on homestead claims. This one was built in the 1880s by George W. Keller, Eldora Muirhead's grandfather, and it is a meticulous and upgraded example of sod houses in the region. Many sod houses were small, one-room dwellings. *Courtesy of Eldora Muirhead and Avis Reddaway.*

cobblers, bakers and laborers figured out every piece of how to survive here for themselves. It's a tenacity that still exists today.

After shelters, gardens were one of the most important improvements to be made for survival on the inhospitable, remote land. As vital as they were to survival, they were not considered an "improvement" to the land and were not reported to land offices when homesteaders filed claims showing that they had "proved up" the land five years later. Crops that could be sold were listed as improvements, but gardens to sustain ranch life seemed a mere fact of it. Some of the early homesteaders came with seeds or plantings to get started, putting in potatoes, corn, carrots, beets and squash. Where low, more soil-stable valleys were present, oats, wheat, corn and sorghum went in.

These crops, if any, were usually planted in small plots, rarely more than forty acres. I looked through hundreds of original homestead claims and read reports of as little as a half an acre of "broken" or tilled ground—just enough for a house, barn, small animal pens and a garden patch. The rest was labeled "unfit for farming" and was grazed by cattle purchased in nascent towns and driven up to the lands. Until homesteaders could grow provisions for themselves, they were dependent on imports dropped at nearby military forts or in new towns. Small herds of ten to twenty cows provided meager income. Horses were purchased as working animals for transportation and to pull mowers and plows to help improve the ground.

Gus Wendler's ledger reveals diverse and unusual plantings in the Sand Hills, such as artichokes and "1894 novelty watermelon," along with staples such as potatoes, squash and string beans. *Courtesy of Dean and Delores Colburn.*

Homesteaders hunted fowl, antelope or deer on land, as well as turtles and fish if they were near water—all of this would be eaten right away since safe food storage wasn't possible. Electricity was a generation or two away.

Grains were milled as needed in a hand-turned grinder. This small grain and coffee mill was a workhorse of an implement in the first kitchens since these staples keep best when stored whole. Coffee was purchased green, or raw, roasted in the home's cast-iron pans and ground for use. Dishes like cornbread were made from freshly milled dried corn; this was an essential dish, since it is forgiving of heat fluctuations while cooking and could be made on the stovetop in a cast-iron skillet with as little as ground corn and wheat, some cream if available and lard.

Stoves for cooking and heat were either brought by covered wagon into the region or purchased when settlers arrived along the way as they passed through areas along Nebraska's settled Missouri riverbanks. They were small, low, cast-iron stovetop varieties that had one small interior chamber for fuel, requiring they be stoked multiple times an hour with a fuel source. The ideal fuel source, coal, was an expensive import. The next best fuel was wood, but the Sand Hills didn't have trees to cut. What was available were fast-burning cow chips (dried cow droppings harvested from pastures), perhaps desirable only because they were free. Corncobs were also free if a crop could be grown and harvested. All cooking was done on the stovetop, so leavened breads were not typically made, and canning was difficult to execute since it involved a large vat of water boiling consistently for twenty to thirty minutes.

When the first wood-framed farmhouses were built on Sand Hills' properties around the turn of the twentieth century, larger, more consistent stoves went into these more permanent kitchens. These stoves usually had a bigger heat chamber, making it possible for higher, consistent heat. They also had separate oven compartments beneath the stovetop. As soon as the oven came into the kitchen, so did leavened breads and the potential to can quantities of food for storage. In the leanest of times on the Great Plains, a kitchen usually had bread, lard and potatoes—enough for sustenance, even if lacking in flavor. Wood-framed houses were built with cellars that served as cold storage, where potatoes, squash, onions, unmilled grains and any cured meats from farm animals like hogs were stored. These frame houses and better kitchen equipment and storage didn't always mean that settlers' diets were improving; that depended on the bounty of the gardens and the opportunity to purchase pantry items like wheat and corn. In winters, diets shrunk considerably, as settlers rationed food to last through the first spring planting and harvest.

In this early wave of settlement, only livestock needed for personal use on the land were kept. There was no irrigation to increase the quantity of grass on the land, so very few cattle could actually be kept on natural forage. (On unimproved, unirrigated Sand Hills land, you need at least ten acres of land per cow for enough forage during the summer. However, you need that same amount of ungrazed land to mow the grasses and store forage for the winter. This effectively requires half of a homestead to be used only for mowing and storing grass, while the other half is used for grazing. Just 640 unimproved acres will reliably support only ten to twenty head of cattle year-round.) Until lands were improved with wells, irrigation, fences, ranch trails and

Not all wood-framed homes were built. Some were towed. This was previously a train boxcar. It was towed by draft horse from a rail yard near Ord, Nebraska, and placed on the family's property in Garfield County. *Courtesy of Owen Long.*

farm equipment, settlers were limited in the number of horses, work animals and cattle that could forage naturally.

Delores's Great Uncle Gus and grandfather Max Wendler were both German immigrants on a later wave of Homestead Act claimants in 1883 and 1907, respectively, behind the flood of American civilians and war veterans continuing to migrate west from the East Coast. By this second influx, settlers were already spread out on the land, and a knowledge of what land was workable was known and commonly shared. Lands that couldn't be tilled were noted at the land office. Plots with small workable patches that could be "broken" for crops were snapped up. Gus kept extremely detailed notes on gardening, noting what he planted and when, down to the hour of the day within the season. His level of detail shows a strategy to diversify plantings within the garden for the best chances of success in these new lands. He planted dozens of types of vegetables every year, adding more of what worked and less of what didn't as the years progressed.

Since gardens were the family's most reliable source of food, they needed to be large enough to feed them for the entire year. One homestead would typically plant a twenty- by twenty-foot space, often twice that for a larger family, usually with a separate, equally sized melon patch for hard and soft squash, melons or any crawling plants that need space to grow. Many gardens had space for experimentation, but the first gardens usually contained, much like they do today, tomatoes, squash, potatoes, peppers, peas and string beans. Summer vegetables like lettuces, celery, rhubarb and strawberries were also prevalent. On any arable land, farmers still planted grains like wheat, corn and oats, as they were viable crops to sell and important food to save for winter months.

The optimism displayed in full-color ads placed by the U.S. government and land offices across the country was real. The desire for Americans and foreigners alike to start over, for free, and the opportunity to become a part of the emerging American dream, full of independence and individual destiny, was also real. But perhaps the most real feature of existence in the Sand Hills was nature itself. These waves of optimism crashed down on soil so sandy it might as well have been a beach without water. The experiences shaped the very language of the homesteaders trying to settle it. The land must be *broken* to make use of it. The prairie winds must be *cut* to slow their powerful temperaments. Winds are *stiff*. Cold is *biting*. Sand is *stinging*. It took an equally strong temperament to match the brutal environment with tenacious resourcefulness, determination and willingness to accept a new definition of optimism tempered by self-sufficiency to cultivate these lands. Other regions of the Great Plains may have demanded this temperament out of its residents, but Sandhillers perfected it. It lives and dies and lives here on the plains today.

NATIVE PEOPLES

The Sand Hills region, like the rest of the country, was occupied by others before the United States' westward expansion. Before the West was settled, it was a vast, open prairie with high plains and untouched mountain ranges. The first cultures didn't approach the land as a grid in sections but rather as areas defined by animal migration, access to water and seasonal changes in weather. Pawnee, Cheyenne and Sioux (among other tribes) were present but did not settle heavily in the Sand Hills. The region was primarily used as tribes' hunting land for migratory bison, following herds into and out of the area on hunts to provide meat and pelts for shelter and clothing.

By the time white settlers started entering the Sand Hills, much of it had already been acquired by the United States in a treaty signed in 1857 with the Pawnee. By then, millions of bison had been systematically slaughtered by U.S. military in efforts to weaken native peoples' dependence on them for sustenance. The Pawnee left all land from north of the Loup River (the southern edge of the Sand Hills) to the South Dakota–Nebraska state line (the north edge of the Sand Hills). Later, the Sioux relinquished their claim to much of the Sand Hills in the Fort Laramie Treaty in 1868. Very few battles in the Sand Hills took place, since by the time westward expansion affected the area, most tribes had already left the land or were forcibly moved to reservations in neighboring states.

The original pattern of native migration through the area was perhaps a predictor of the settlement challenges to come. A fundamental difference in perception and treatment of the land was evident in European-American expansion and settlement of the United States. These perfectly square sections of land doled out disregarded existing residents, as well as climate, environment, experience with the geography and natural resources. It was blind to the attributes of certain types of land; parcels near water tended to be more arable, and thus valuable, than land far away from a water source.

When the tribes lost their homelands and hunting grounds, knowledge of existing edible plants and animals that would sustain small populations went with them. Native edible foods on the land—such as wild oats on riverbanks, sand cherries, chokecherries, mulberries, sorrel, wild grapes, strawberries, asparagus, gourds, wild onions and plums—needed to be rediscovered. In the high plains and westernmost Sand Hills, prickly pear paddles and their fruit, when found on the plains, were scraped, skinned and eaten. Yucca root, a filling, valuable starch, was dug up, cooked and eaten, and it is still commonly found in the high plains and Sand Hills. Wild medicinal herbs such as Echinacea (coneflower) and dandelion root were identified, harvested and used for medicinal purposes. New American settlers started new lives and their own struggles for survival without the benefit of local, resident knowledge about food and other crucial survival techniques.

Today, the Mari Sandoz Center in Chadron has gardens dedicated to educating visitors about native Sand Hills plants and orchards, as well as the first permanent settler plantings. The "Immigrant Garden" is full of plants taken from abandoned homesteads of the early permanent settlers.

The permanent settlers had arrived. But life in the Sand Hills wasn't easy, and it wasn't working. It took the Railroad Act to convince people to come into the most remote part of the Great American Desert.

RAILROADS AND EXPANSION

Chugging along right behind the Homestead Act came the most important industrial creation of the time. Just six months after the passage of the act, the Railroad Act of 1862 became law. The U.S. government was a supporter of settlement, and the railroads would help expand and claim the rest of the continent—both needed customers along this emerging network to buy, sell and ship things that required coast-to-coast transportation. Increased transportation meant increased access to provisions and a more robust economy.

To deliver on their part of the promise, every affected state or territory across the country gave the railroads wide swaths of land easements on either side of the planned routes for the railroad companies to create this new economy around the rails. The territory of Nebraska was no exception, giving Union Pacific Railroad twenty-mile-wide swaths on either side of the tracks, amounting to about 16 percent of the state's total land. A less charitable view of the Railroad Act suggests that the act itself set off one of the first corporate land grabs of the new country. Some of this land granted to the railroads to use, or sell, however they pleased was already settled by new immigrants. (The phrase "railroaded" evolved from this period of rapid acquisition and resale of land to mean something along the lines of hasty, oppressive action for which there has not been enough time to object.)

Union Pacific Railroads implemented "emigrant fares"—reduced-fare one-way tickets in essentially empty boxcars fitted for utilitarian passenger transport to various stops along the way for the purpose of relocating oneself and one's family. One could also buy a ticket to the "end of road," which in 1868 was Omaha. As the race to complete the transcontinental railroad progressed, these "end of road" fares extended to places west like Grand Island, Kearney and North Platte. By May 10, 1869, the final spike in the coast-to-coast route had been driven into the ground, and a new way of looking at the country and its opportunities began. Texas cattlemen driving their herds up to station stops in the late 1860s to ship to the larger market doubled their market to points west.

For provisions and food, the completion of the transcontinental railroad opened a whole new world of available ingredients. From the East came tins of oysters, sardines, canned seafood and vegetables. From the West, produce from California's fertile Central Valley. Citrus traveled well without refrigeration, and in the right times of year, so did grapes. One of the first documented shipments of refrigerated food was in 1872 by a strawberry grower in Cobden, Illinois. He built a refrigerated wooden boxcar with a V-shaped ice bunker suspended from the roof of the car to hold the ice. Its shipment of strawberries traveled a short distance from central Illinois to Chicago. The shipment was a success, and later experiments of meat and butter shipped between New York State and Boston solidified the idea and served to create the demand for these products. In 1906, Union Pacific, holding the vast majority of railways across the North American continent that would become the United States, decided to enter into the refrigerated car market and contracted a company to build refrigerated cars for cross-country transports. This collaboration became the Pacific Fruit Express, with trains originating in bountiful California. The door was open for commerce, and Sand Hills settlers would soon have access to ingredients they had only previously dreamed of.

However, it would be ten years after the first experimental iced shipment that the Sand Hills even received a rail line. Sand Hills residents now had some access points to goods that were becoming available in other regions of the country. Union Pacific Railroads advertised prices on handbills for items that could be shipped by rail, such as butter, lard, soap, ceramic crocks for food storage, canned goods, liquor, tobacco, books, blankets, hardware, tools, glass and wagon parts. For all the importance placed on shipping ingredients *into* the area, shipping ingredients *out* was just as valuable to both. The system was at its most efficient when every boxcar arriving, when unloaded, was loaded with goods to ship out of the area.

Eldora Muirhead was born in 1921 in Cascade, a now unincorporated town in Cherry County, and so is too young to remember when the trains came to Valentine in 1883. But she remembers the commerce and products that it brought into and out of the region, as well as when the last train rolled out of Valentine in 1992. As a child, she remembers men cutting ice out of the rivers to load into boxcars to ship to Omaha. The ice was sawed into blocks, dragged out of the Niobrara, put in boxcars waiting in Valentine and shipped back to Omaha. Sometimes, the ice was packed around a product, and sometimes the ice itself was the commodity. Cities loved fresh meats, so cottage industries for products like dressed chickens, shipped on ice, sprung up on ranches near the railroad. At that time, a chicken that had already spent two days on ice was considered one of poor quality, but it was still useful income for ranch women, so not many questions were asked. Even today, Eldora can't make sense of why people would want to buy a two- or three-day-dead animal to eat. One thing the Sand Hills farms and ranches had grown accustomed to was fresh ingredients, as rare as they were at the time.

In 1879, Eldora's grandfather George W. Keller rode an emigrant car west to Omaha from Pennsylvania with his pregnant wife and four kids. They made it out to Cherry County, where he ultimately acquired upward of 4,000 acres about thirty miles south of Valentine, Nebraska, near the township of Cascade. Ranching was his main operation, although roughly 150 acres—a fairly large amount—was reserved for farming food that he needed for his growing family. The North Loup River ran through his acreage. A river close to one's land usually meant that drilling a well for water would be a shallow endeavor, perhaps as little as twenty feet, whereas dry land settlements might have to go as deep as three hundred feet. From the nearby river, the family was able to fish, pull ice in the winters for preserving foods and have access to an unlimited supply of fresh, cool water. Rivers also usually brought with them swaths of nutrient-rich, fertile soil to their valleys.

One of George's sons and Eldora's father, John Fishburn Keller, remained on that land, and he and his wife, Nelda, raised their family and worked the ranch until 1948, when they sold it to two of Eldora's brothers for twelve dollars per acre. "It was the only time I ever saw my mother cry," Eldora told me. "She said to the boys, 'You'll be in debt for the rest of your lives.'" The brothers put in irrigation to help grow more grass on the land and built up a profitable cattle business. Decades later, they sold their holdings for "a lot of money" and retired to Steamboat Springs, Colorado.

The recipes to make foods from all these new products available by rail made an incalculable difference in the kitchens and on ranch tables in

The beauty of utility: someone turned old wire hangers into a utensil rack for the kitchen. Stephanie Bixby Graham found the rack in an abandoned homestead. It now hangs in her restored schoolhouse turned Sand Hills history archive and holds her collection of vintage utensils.

the Sand Hills. Early cookbooks arrived in the region with settlers from the East Coast and were usually large, all-purpose volumes like the *Boston Cooking School Cook Book, Mrs. Lincoln's Boston Cookbook* and the popular *Fannie Farmer Cookbook*, all published in the 1890s. They contained many recipes Sandhillers simply couldn't make because the ingredients weren't available in the interior country. The railroads changed that predicament, bringing crocks or cans of lard, canned vegetables and fruits, yeast, spices both basic and exotic and kitchen utensils. Luxury ingredients like tins of oysters, smoked fish and sardines appeared in general stores. Whether settlers could afford them or not was a different story.

The first wave of settlers was enticed by the United States government, advertising free land to Civil War veterans and people in the East. The second wave of later migration—the wave Gus Wendler was on—started in the 1880s, when the railroads began their advertising campaigns to sell the lands granted to them by the government to people abroad. These corporations reached beyond U.S. shores and launched successful ad campaigns across eastern and western European countries. Poles, Bohemians, Czechs, Germans, Swedes, Danes, Scots, Irish and Dutch emigrated in waves in search of free land that promised the opportunity to start new lives and communities, many hoping for freedom from political and religious prosecution.

Entire towns created from an ethnic identity—like Polish Loup City, Danish Dannebrog and Czech Wilber—all exist outside the Sand Hills. Inside the sandy border, collections of various affiliations within the Sand Hills didn't take the shape of entire villages but rather collections of people into "settlements" or "hills," such as the "Polish hills" outside Burwell. There was a similar collection of ancestral Bohemians in Garfield County. Outside Valentine in Cherry County, a "German settlement" formed, another tight-knit collection of farmers. People today still use these identifiers to describe the geographical regions. Custer County has a thriving Irish population but no settled town to call its own.

Typically, immigrants entered through main ports on the eastern seaboard, making the now well-traveled journey west in search of new homes. With them they brought traditions and foods not seen in the Sand Hills. Germans brought the savory *runza*, a meat and sauerkraut pastry that originated in Russia but spread and was quickly adopted by Germany, and the sweet *kuchen*, the German word for "cake." Danes brought the pastry we now call "Danish," but a traditional pastry, *aebelskiver*, kept its original name and didn't fall under a generic moniker. *Aebelskiver*, while requiring a bit of technique to make the puffed pancake, was easy to make, and the fact that it requires a special pan gives it a distinctive mark of culture and community. A hallmark of Czechoslovakian (and regional Bohemian) immigrants is the addition of poppy seeds to pastry. Much more plentiful then than now, a simple *makový dort* (whole poppy seed cake) calls for a cup of poppy seeds, soaked overnight in milk to soften.

Perhaps the most renowned and revered Czech recipe is for *kolace*. This well-known pastry recipe may have survived the journey abroad if only because the main ingredients used to make it were readily available in the Sand Hills (and the Great Plains at large). This egg dough's middle is dotted with a sweet filling and baked. The filling would change with fruits available in the region, but *kolace* were able to be made year-round with cheese fillings, perhaps while the cook was waiting for a shipment of plums or poppy seeds to make the traditional versions. Making these foods in new lands was the easiest way to bring a sense of place and belonging to the New World. It created an identity, a cohesion and a reminder of cultural roots, of home and a sense of community to foreign land in the process of becoming "home."

Settlers and immigrants alike often brought loose collections of family recipes, many originals of which are lost today. Early cookbooks weren't in production in the region, so recipes were written by hand on scraps of paper and tucked into the backs of the one or two cookbooks imported to the area. Recipes like sauerbraten, blood sausage, sauerkraut, cakes, breads and pies were made so often they were usually prepared from memory. When traditional ingredients became available—like poppy seeds for *kolace* filling—women made these recipes as close to their originals as possible, providing small but mighty salves for any homesickness. Today, single-recipe festivals abound as a connecting point with community and a reflection of pride of heritage. Although not in the Sand Hills itself, the annual "Kolace Shoot-Out" is held in Elba and draws more than eight hundred eager visitors from around the state annually. This number is four times the size of the town itself.

As for the rails, small spur lines sprung up in the Sand Hills in the 1880s and 1890s, creating valuable inroads to remote areas. Lines into Burwell, Sargent, Broken Bow and Stapleton touched the Sand Hills to the south. In the north, stops in Atkinson, Long Pine, Ainsworth, Valentine, Gordon and Rushville reached the top of the Sand Hills. This might help explain why ethnic groups did not settle entire towns in the interior Sand Hills since other areas were more accessible places to catch the wave of westward immigration. In 1887, the *Mullen Roundup*, a bound compilation of the area's history, reported that the Grand Island and Wyoming Railroad built a line into Hooker County through what is now Mullen. This is the only line that traverses the middle of the Sand Hills, following historic Highway 2 through the Nebraska National Forest, through Thedford, on through to Ellsworth and into Alliance. In Ellsworth, the stop on the line became the site of the historic Spade Ranch store, set up to house provisions needed to operate the massive ranch. The building opened for retail sales in 1897 and still operates today, next to the railroad tracks, which are still in heavy operation, although it no longer receives goods from the line.

These lines and provisions changed kitchen work for the better. One of Eldora's first childhood memories of food was of her mother's cake: "I remember this and cinnamon rolls my mother would make every time she made a batch of bread." It's an adaptable recipe that starts with a plain vanilla cake. Even plain, it made a lasting impact on her as a child; Eldora recited this cake from memory eighty years after she remembers her mother making it for her. There were three versions altogether: plain, chocolate and lemon. The cocoa powder Eldora's mother used in her all-purpose cake would have been shipped from points in the East. "The chocolate cake was rather dry, as I remember it," she says. "But when you're feeding it to a bunch of kids with whipped cream on it, we didn't care!" When refrigerated cars containing citrus came from the West in about 1910, they were able to make lemon cake with fresh lemons. Thirty years earlier, neither was possible in the region.

Eldora's Lemon Cake

Eldora doesn't look a day over eighty, and at the young age of ninety-three, she can still rattle off recipes from long-ago memories in Cherry County ranch kitchens, including measurements, methods and brands like Watkins vanilla. I scribbled these recollections in my notebook and decided to search for the same ingredients that she and her mother would have used in the 1920s and 1930s to test them. Watkins vanilla is still widely available in grocery stores and online. But the cream these early permanent settlers had to work with was raw. The journey to find my own raw, unseparated milk to bake with took a week of asking around in grocery stores and cafés in the Sand Hills. One evening, sitting around the "old-timers" table at the bar in the basement of the American Legion club in Burwell, someone recalled knowing a man about thirty-five miles outside of town who still milks his own dairy cows. I tracked him down, and on his next trip into town, he left me a gallon of cream. Since selling raw milk is technically not legal, I *donated* some money to his cows. With it, I began testing all of the recipes in the book that contain cream to note the difference. (His cows received a few donations over the months.)

Cake, like most other recipes in our kitchens, has evolved with time. In the early pioneer days, the 1850s, many sweeteners at the time were made from sorghum or barley, and cakes were denser and less sweet in part due to the weight of these thick liquids. Today, crystallized cane sugar is as common as table salt, changing our palates to desire lighter and sweeter pastry. Eldora's mother's recipe calls for lighter granulated sugar and originally used raw "top milk," the heavy cream that separates to the top of the jar. (The closest equivalent today is the pasteurized heavy whipping cream found on store shelves.) The result is a flavorful, dense, sweet cake, closer in texture to a muffin.

This lemon cake is a modest adaptation of the original, which is to say it is gently brought forward into history using lighter cream and more lemon. Its texture is muffin-like, but its simplicity shines because of its historical reference point. It is adapted for use with pasteurized half-and-half cream, which is far more widely available to us than a gallon of raw milk. Using lemon as the citrus provides the best "zing." (I baked this cake with grapefruit and a Meyer lemon as comparisons.) After so many tests, I can almost hear Eldora laughing at me for spending so much time to decide that the best version of this cake ends up being so close to the original, denser cake. If you have the opportunity to use raw milk, please use it one-for-one as a substitution for the half-and-half in this recipe. You will not be disappointed.

This cake, in Eldora's own words, is adaptable. The plain version contains just vanilla. A lemon variety adds lemon zest and the juice of one lemon. Chocolate added to the mix indeed has a drying effect on the cake recipe, exactly as Eldora remembers. You can add a fourth of a cup of the best cocoa powder available (I tested with Valrhona chocolate) and bake it for a little less time. It should be eaten warm with a nice dollop of whipped cream. It doesn't hold well overnight. Even so, the versatility of this recipe reveals a true pioneer spirit, making the most of what women had in the kitchen and interchanging ingredients to keep things interesting. From this one recipe, three flavors of cake can be made.

••

ELDORA'S LEMON CAKE
Serves: 8–10

INGREDIENTS
2 cups flour, sifted
1 cup sugar
2 teaspoons baking powder
3 large, fresh eggs

1 tablespoon vanilla (*Watkins pure double-strength*
   extract preferred)
1 cup ½ & ½ cream
zest and juice of one lemon (about 2 tablespoons juice)

METHOD

Preheat oven to 375°F. In one bowl, combine and whisk dries through a sifter. (Add cocoa powder to this bowl if using; see below.) In a separate bowl, add eggs, vanilla and cream and whisk together with lemon juice and zest if using. Pour the wets into the dries and quickly mix together with a spatula, only until combined. Immediately pour into a greased 8x8-inch baking pan and put in the oven. After 20 minutes, reduce the heat to 350°F, open the door to turn the pan and bake for another 25–30 minutes or until a toothpick comes out clean, for a total of 45–50 minutes. Remove from oven, and after five minutes, unmold from the pan and remove cake to a cooling rack. Slice into squares, dust with powdered sugar, top with fresh whipped cream and berries (optional) and serve.

FOR VANILLA CAKE: *Omit the lemon above and bake per lemon cake.*

FOR CHOCOLATE CAKE: *Add ¼ cup cocoa powder to the dry mix and reduce the baking time to 375°F for 20 minutes, after which you reduce heat to 350°F and bake for an additional 20–25 minutes, for a total of 40–45 minutes.*

The railroads' incisions proved to be lifelines into the Sand Hills and are telltale signs of the settlement of the region. Even with all these benefits to settlers, railroads and farmers had a delicate relationship. The more farmers prospered, the more product they were able to ship out via rail, generating more farm income; this, in turn, theoretically meant that there was more money to spend on products that could be shipped into towns. This was the justification the railroads used to acquire free land to build their businesses—that it was in *everyone's* best interest to cultivate community and the land that would produce goods to distribute throughout the transportation system. Until the automobile took hold more than thirty years later, in terms of influence, the theory worked, and it was full steam ahead into settling the Great Plains. There was just one problem: the homesteaders who were settling the Great Plains were still struggling to make a living off the land.

TIMBER CULTURE ACT OF 1873

In a time of such boundless optimism, encouraged by free land from the Homestead Act and the completion of the first coast-to-coast railroad, it hardly seemed possible that the Sand Hills would be some of the most difficult land to tame. The high turnover of homesteads indicated a few things: owners were failing to make the land productive and were selling their claims to other homesteaders, or claims were being abandoned as people moved out of the area to find better land. Both were true, and there were also many stories of fraudulent claims in attempts to grab more land in between. The Timber Culture Act of 1873 was a small token of assistance to flailing homesteaders. It allowed eligible homesteaders to take an additional quarter section (160 acres) to supplement their existing homesteads provided they plant a certain percentage of it with trees. This act was passed to help "settle" the land with physical roots.

Trees were essential first improvements made in the Sand Hills anyway. Nurseries from both east and west shipped bare root trees and seeds that settlers used to plant for wind protection, food and shade. Trees added much-needed cover, gave the soil strength, broke up the strong prairie winds, provided harvestable food, added beauty and helped establish the feeling of a real town, neighborhood or homestead with each planting. They are an especially sentimental symbol in the Sand Hills because chances are if you see a tree, someone planted it by hand. Planting came right behind building; after gardens, trees were typically the next things a town or homesteader put in once structures were built.

Delores's Great Uncle Gus was able to expand his land by filing for a timber claim. The trees he planted to honor the claim in 1883 still stand on the ranch today. His attempt was successful, but for many, even with an original 160 acres from the Homestead Act, the additional 160 acres from a "timber claim" was not nearly enough to sustain a family. It never was, but it didn't stop lawmakers from trying to keep settlers in the Sand Hills.

KINKAID ACT OF 1904

After forty years of various Homestead Act and Timber Culture claims, failures and broken spirits, Nebraska congressman and Sand Hills resident Moses Kinkaid decided to try to solve the settlement problem in the Sand

Hills once and for all. In 1902, Kinkaid became a district representative for the Sixth Nebraska District in the House of Representatives, a region that comprised almost the entirety of the Sand Hills. By the time he took office, it was well established that homesteaders could not "prove up" on a mere 160 acres of sand and grass. As the homesteaders he represented in the region failed, Kinkaid proposed expanding the Homestead Act in this area to 640 acres, presuming that more land offered homesteaders more opportunity to succeed. The act passed in 1904 and created a new wave of settlers, called "Kinkaiders," to the Sand Hills to settle. Any unclaimed lands west of the 98th meridian in Nebraska were made available to be claimed in either full sections or 640-acre plots.

On paper, the act was considered a success. The Sand Hills region was settled. More than 9 million new acres of the Sand Hills were claimed, and by 1917, almost all the available land had been spoken for. In reality, it still wasn't enough land to ranch on, and the act was subject to as many (if not more) fraudulent claims as was the Homestead Act. Nevertheless, Kinkaid remained a representative of the Sixth District until his death in 1922 and was largely seen as a successful politician who gave Sand Hills residents new life. There were other acts that modified the Homestead Act, but the Kinkaid Act was the only one that truly set the Sand Hills apart from the rest of the state and the Great Plains.

While the Kinkaid Act was a step in the right direction, even still, 640 acres was not enough to be able to make a living in the region. Remembering that 640 acres is only enough land to raise ten to fifteen cows to a profitable weight without the addition of bringing in extra hay for feed or irrigating the land, at a market rate of about $1,000 per cow today, that's hardly enough income to live on. Many homesteaders cobbled together claims from the Homestead Act, the Timber Culture Act and the Kinkaid Act, and those who could get footholds on the land purchased more to increase their holdings. Often times, they mortgaged their herds and their horses to do it.

In Sand Hills kitchens, one of the first domestic successes was a compilation of recipes published in a cookbook in the Wood Lake region in 1904, one of the first cookbooks of and by the Sand Hills. In it, hints of successful towns and homesteads are apparent with recipes that make use of imported tins of food like oysters and other rail-delivered luxuries. Even with these delicacies available, most of the recipes are ones of economy and utility.

A more common recipe found in the book was for a "Short-Cake" recipe, a simple, sweet treat and a fantastic example of unwritten knowledge—the "use your judgment" technique that exists in kitchens everywhere then and now. There is no temperature indication or duration of cooking, and there is no measure for the amount of flour:

••

SHORT-CAKE

2 cups sour cream
2–3 teaspoons soda
2 teaspoons Royal Baking Powder
pinch salt
flour to make soft dough

Roll thin and spread with butter. Fold together and bake quickly. When done, unfold and spread fruit in between and on top.

Eldora's mother's copy of the Wood Lake cookbook is on display at Cherry County Historical Society in Valentine.

In the early 1900s, what are now pantry basics like flour, meat and milk were still scarce, forcing families to survive on any garden bounty that could be overwintered, like root vegetables in cellars and any canned fresh vegetables that could be preserved. In the Cherry County family history "Only Yesterday," the author remembers as a young girl an extremely difficult winter when they didn't even have flour, forcing her mother to send a traveling cowboy on to the next house, a notable break in plains spirit. (Typical plains hospitality at the time would feed travelers who approached ranches and offer a night's stay if it was too late to press forward in their journeys.)

For Sand Hills families who were having trouble establishing their claims, the winter months were the hardest, as they drained the last of the root vegetables and jarred foods. Trapping rodents like beaver; hunting blackbirds, frogs and turtles; and fishing for bullhead provided sustenance, but few, if any, recipes survive from these dark times—turtle soup would have been turtle meat boiled in water. When spring plantings could go in, June brought peas, carrots and potatoes. July brought sweet corn, and August brought tomatoes. The bounty of summer was evident in the grocery list— only beans, bacon, flour, yeast, sugar, salt, coffee and tea were purchased to supplement the summer months.

Most of the recipes in books at this point were ones of utility; the tinned oyster bake was a rare sight. But even utility in recipes indicated improvement in conditions. It meant that there were enough ingredients to work with to have options. The common egg regularly and repeatedly proved its value on the farm, stretching more expensive ingredients like cheese, such as in the following recipe from the Wood Lake cookbook for cheese sandwiches: "Rub yolks of three hard-boiled eggs smooth, mix in very slowly two teaspoons oil, stirring with a fork. Add a little mustard, cayenne pepper and salt and one tablespoon vinegar. When thoroughly mixed add one cup grated cheese."

All sorts of adjustments on farms and ranches were being made, inside and out of the kitchens. But for these kitchens, railroads brought more provisions in and allowed for revenue streams to be generated out, giving women more options within their domains. And onward settlers went into the '20s and '30s of the twentieth century.

In 1910, there were 129,678 Nebraska farms listed in the USDA Census of Agriculture.

FOOD PRESERVATION

O ur refrigerator was the north window in the kitchen," Irene Nelson Walker tells me. She was born in 1930 and has lived her entire life in Garfield County, raising her family here in the Sand Hills. She now lives with her daughter, Tammy, and son-in-law, Jerry Rowse. She fondly remembers life on the "home place," north of the Rowses' ranch. Just last year, her children treated her to a flight over the homestead that Irene grew up on for her birthday. "Now, it's just a little shack, sticking its head out of the trees." But in the 1930s, the house seemed huge, and the Sand Hills were her playground. She vividly recalls only having one doll growing up, but it didn't matter—the real fun was out back of the house at the top of the sandy hill. She and friends from town would roll down it for hours, coming inside sandy and tired. Many times, she'd find her mother in the kitchen, canning "anything she could get her hands on."

By the time Irene was a young child, the waves of homestead claimants slowed, and their successes and failures in the Sand Hills were becoming apparent. So much of the ability to tolerate life in the region depended on good judgment, especially in the kitchen. Good use and knowing when things were about to spoil or when they were ripe, done or ready was key to knowing when to can, or "put up" cans, for the winter. Knowing how and where to butcher, process and store a hog became innate knowledge if it wasn't already. Kitchens were creating, preparing and storing food to keep pace with growing families and ranches.

CELLARS

Cellars are remarkably efficient food preservation methods for doing so little as digging a deep hole in the ground. A cellar six feet below ground in the summer will stay cool at around sixty degrees and in winter will often remain right at freezing. In the 1920s, before iceboxes and refrigerators, these were the main pantry storage facilities, and many farm and ranch houses still use them today. Originally, thick five- and ten-pound ceramic crocks were used to store salted slabs of pork, large batches of pickled vegetables and cream.

These crude walk-in refrigerators contained any number of different preservation methods within them. Eldora remembers her mother's "fifteen-day pickles," brined, unheated pickles usually made with cucumbers from the garden, soaked in a vinegar solution and weighted down in crocks. Her family also had some "uptown" (or "impressive," in Sand Hills parlance) cellar storage. Her father routed a pipe from the nearby windmill through one side of the cellar wall. This water fed into a trough that was built a few feet off the ground and ran the length of the cellar. A pipe on the other end routed the water out of the cellar. Eldora remembers seeing cream cans bobbling in the trough, everything in it cooled by the constant running water. "Cream would stay good for a couple of days in that setup," a long time in the days before mechanical refrigeration.

This is the house in which Eldora Muirhead grew up. The windmill in the back pumped into the basement, which fed water into a trough and out the side door as a way to keep perishable foods like dairy cool. *Courtesy of Eldora Muirhead and Avis Reddaway.*

SANDBOXES

Many Sandhillers remember that the sandboxes in the cellars were not to play in but rather to store the season's supply of carrots, onions, potatoes and other root vegetables grown in the gardens. Submerging recently harvested root vegetables in a box of clean, dampened sand is an efficient method of pushing them into dormancy for food preservation. The Sand Hills has an endless supply of fine, clean sand, and pioneers learned to make good use of it. Leaving the root hairs intact on the vegetables and submerging the vegetables in sand, leaving just the closely trimmed stems peeking out of the surface, can preserve vegetables for up to six months. Families who could put up enough could have root vegetables through the winter and spring.

CISTERNS

"We didn't have a refrigerator when we moved here." Delores looks out the window and points, saying, "I had a windmill down there and piped it into an upright tank, and you put the butter and the cream and the milk in a jar. I'm sure you've heard that a lot." Cisterns, windmill catchment tanks, were invaluable on ranches. Delores used hers well into the 1950s. These tanks captured water for cattle and people and were a valuable source of food preservation until refrigeration became available. Melvin Hyde, born in Loup County in 1930 on a dry land farm, remembers his walk up the hill to the cistern to fetch cream from the can tied to the edge. Eldora recalls that their cream would stay fresh in temperate months for up to forty-eight hours in water, almost twice the time it would typically remain usable.

ICEHOUSES

In the Sand Hills, people don't make a habit of calling things "valuable," opting instead for "useful" or "helpful." Ice is no exception to this. Ice had very little monetary value on ranches, yet it was one of the most useful items in the kitchen. In winter, when rivers and ponds froze solid, teams of men and horses would travel to the ice and saw huge blocks, removing and transporting them to private or community icehouses. In Valentine, ice became a cottage industry that emerged at the Niobrara River in winter. Men sawed blocks of ice to transport them directly onto boxcars, which were then shipped to Omaha. (Here, ice did have some value as a commodity sold to the railroads.) Locally, community icehouses were large storage areas, often collaboratively built by a few different ranches or by the towns they served. They operated in honor code fashion; patrons took only what they needed. Ice was kept frozen by covering it with layers of hay, and oftentimes the icehouses were partially below ground for extra insulation.

If the ice was well covered through a mild summer, it would keep until July, leaving only three or four months of the year without this method of food preservation. "We could have ice cream for the Fourth of July most years," Eldora says. Her family had their own icehouse next to the adjoining river. Melvin recalls traveling to one of Loup County's community icehouses near the river for ice on his family's farm. He recalls having ice into June. In both cases, ice was a luxury, and families spent many hot, dry summer months without its benefits.

ICEBOXES

What people remember most about iceboxes is not always the convenience they brought to kitchens. Sandhillers remember how terribly they leaked. These heavy, wooden, non-mechanical cabinets contained a metal interior compartment at the top that held a block of ice and a metal pan at the bottom to catch the water. In between was cool air, where vegetables, meats and dairy could be stored. Retailers had recommended organizational schemes for the shelves: dairy and meats on the bottom, to which the cold air sank, and vegetables at the top. Iceboxes had a heyday from the 1900s to 1930s and were perhaps the kitchen's first item of conspicuous consumption; many models were also attractive pieces of furniture worthy of display. But the utility was also felt. Women were able to store perishable items upstairs in the kitchen, preventing the need to constantly run up and down cellar stairs for food. Outside of summer months, an ice block could remain frozen for a week, giving food a larger window to stay usable. Since original farmhouse kitchens were very small and not built with expansion in mind, oftentimes iceboxes were placed in adjoining dining rooms. If you ever see original wooden floors water damaged in dining rooms, this is probably why.

CANNING

"I remember the first money I made as a married woman," Eldora tells me. "A woman from town came out to our ranch and wanted cucumbers that were all the same size for canning." She gave Eldora a fifty-cent piece for a couple bushels of small pickling cucumbers and went on her way. Eldora went inside, found a safety pin and scratched that day's date into the fifty-cent piece. She still has the coin today.

Canning did not usually provide a direct income like Eldora was proud to receive that day. A pantry full of canned goods contained its own value and still does in today's kitchens. Eldora recalls that during the days of ceramic crocks in the cellar, her mother cooked large slices of pork along with fatty bacon, placed the meat in jars and poured the grease over the meats. As the fat cooled, it sealed the meat, preventing air from reaching it. This concept is also known as "confit," from the French word *confire*, which means "to preserve." The French commonly made confit with duck, cooking it all in the same container in which it was served or cooled.

Isla Emerton was impressed by her mother canning in two-quart jars, a very large size at the time and an indication of how much bounty their garden produced. With five children on the farm, large meals were common and necessary. "You were supposed to be cautious of green beans," but in her ninety-three years, Eldora cannot think of a time anyone she knew became sick from home canning. "If it was spoiled, you knew it by the time you got the can open," Eldora remembers. "You'd see it, the mold, or smell it. You just knew it and wouldn't eat it."

In 1920, there were 124,417 Nebraska farms listed in the USDA Census of Agriculture.

SAND HILLS CUISINE EMERGES

About one mile onto Dean and Delores's ranch, the road turns from soft clay gravel to oil, or hard-surfaced blacktop. These four miles of blacktop were built by the state on the ranch in 1964 to address complaints by the Colburn family that recreational hunters and fishermen were eroding the Colburns' pastures. Crossing their ranch was the best way to gain access to a lake just beyond it called Beaver Lake. Tire tracks across a Sand Hills pasture create deep indentations in the land, exposing the bare sand. Once the tracks were worn in, the deep rifts would create a clearance problem for cars. Tourists would then create another set of tracks next to the original set, leaving multiple open wounds on the pasture that the Colburns still rely on to graze their cattle. On these delicate Sand Hills, tire tracks expose the sand, creating a dangerous opportunity for the prairie winds to catch the raw sand and start eroding the hills, causing disastrous "blow-outs." Exposed, loose sand is very difficult to stop once started, since it is also very difficult to plant anything in such sandy soil. This fact is largely why the Sand Hills as a grassland remained intact through the Dust Bowl of the 1930s, when overplowing the land eroded topsoil, which blew away in large areas of the Great Plains.

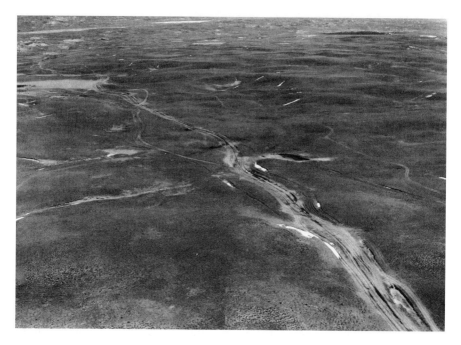

Aerial photo of Dean and Delores Colburn's ranch, showing the destruction to pasture caused by visitors to neighboring lakes. *Courtesy of Dean and Delores Colburn.*

FISH FOR BREAKFAST

Despite pasture damage, the traffic was once a welcome sight on the ranch. In 1930, to supplement ranch income and also provide a little fun, Delores's Great Uncle Gus started a "fish camp," a recreational fishing and hunting camp on one of the ranch's lakes. (Hunting lodges are a legacy that perseveres today in the Sand Hills, attracting an international crowd for trophy fowl and game hunting in the wildlife-rich area.) Even though Uncle Gus started the camp during the Great Depression, it soared in popularity. Fishermen (and women) and hunters from as far away as Omaha came to enjoy the beauty and bounty that the Sand Hills provided. They hunted ducks, geese, prairie chicken and grouse and fished in the natural lakes that the Ogalalla Aquifer's high water table creates in the porous Sand Hills. Great Uncle Gus fed and provided ample recreation for tourists, renting boats and housing them in canvas tents on the land. While much of the hunting was for sport, many of the ducks and geese taken off the land were used for meals.

A large haul of waterfowl at the fish camp on the Wendler Ranch, circa 1935. *Courtesy of Dean and Delores Colburn.*

This point in time reveals an interesting transition for fish as an ingredient. Before electric refrigeration, fish was commonly eaten for the first next meal after it was caught. Since fishing is usually best at dawn and dusk, it typically happened right after supper or immediately before breakfast. As a result, fish was typically served for breakfast. It was cleaned, gutted, pan-fried and eaten whole or broken up into a hash of eggs and potatoes. Farmers and ranchers lucky enough to be near rivers set trout lines across them or fished with rods. Ranch hands out on large ranches with lakes would fish during overnight treks out on the property tending cows and cook the fish over campfires, chuck wagon–style. Catfish, trout, pike, bluegill, bullhead and crappie were all common fish; they were even more common before dams went in along rivers.

Delores's grandmother Ida and Great Uncle Gus would cook for campers, preparing fish pulled right out of the lake. She and Gus would not have known then that they were on the pioneering side of creating Sand Hills cuisine, making something tasty out of just a few simple ingredients. What makes Sand Hills recipes unique, regardless of their origins, is how simply the ingredients are used, as well as the simplicity in their preparation.

Recipes that became workhorses in kitchens needed to fulfill a few key requirements. They needed to be versatile. One recipe could easily be doubled, tripled or halved without many adjustments. Sand Hills recipes also had to be adaptable. Substitutions for ingredients or amounts in these early settlement years were a necessity since garden bounty was dependent on successful growing seasons. Pantries also ran dry depending on the time of year and amount of money on the ranch. If one didn't have any baking powder, an egg would need to work as a leavener, and the recipes needed to support the change. Recipes with beef needed to be able to support a substitution of pork. And finally, recipes had to be "masters." One recipe needed to do a number of things, especially in baking. The same base recipe was regularly adjusted into different flavors, shapes and sizes. The recipes that survive are much like the people who use them: sturdy, no-nonsense, industrious, make-do types. The act of making the recipe itself is what makes it special—a "special" recipe might be simply "showing off." The thoughtfulness of a regular recipe, made well, will do just fine in the Sand Hills.

· ·

GUS'S BREAKFAST HASH
Serves: 2

Inspired by the fish camp, I named this recipe after Great Uncle Gus and the place he ran for years on the ranch.

INGREDIENTS
4 medium potatoes (about 1 pound), scrubbed
1 whole trout or small freshwater whitefish such as perch or crappie (about 1½ pounds), cleaned and gutted, with head and tail removed
6 eggs
2 tablespoons oil or bacon grease
salt and pepper to taste

METHOD
For potatoes in oven: If using an oven, preheat to 350°F and place potatoes directly onto wire racks. Bake for 45 minutes or until a fork easily pierces the flesh. Remove from oven and let potatoes cool to the touch. Chop potatoes into ½-inch cubes and set aside.

For potatoes in embers: Place the potatoes in the center of a large piece of heavy-duty aluminum foil. Place 1 tablespoon bacon grease on top and fold the ends and top of the foil to make a packet, securing tightly so steam does not escape. Place this packet in active campfire embers for 30 minutes. Remove from embers and let potatoes cool to the touch. Chop potatoes into ½-inch cubes and set aside.

For the fish: Melt 1 tablespoon bacon grease or oil in a 12-inch skillet on medium heat. When shimmering, place the fish in the center of the skillet, cover the skillet and do not check it for five minutes. Carefully flip with a spatula, cover and sauté again for another five minutes. Check a piece for doneness—the flesh should be white all the way through. Remove from pan and let cool to the touch. When workable, remove the skin from the flesh and as many bones as you can with your fingers; then gently break up into bite-sized pieces, checking for bones.

Return the skillet to medium heat, scraping and removing any skin that might have gotten stuck. Add a teaspoon of bacon grease or oil, and when shimmering, add six eggs to the pan, stirring continuously. Cook until the eggs are soft but firm, about four minutes. Add potatoes and fish in the last minute of cooking. Serve with coffee and enjoy.

Based on all the photos I saw at Delores's of the fish camp, I bet Gus would have loved a side of duck bacon with this hash.

POULTRY

Fish was a common recreational ingredient in the Sand Hills, but the staple on tables came from a source much closer to home. Isla Emerton was born in a farmhouse west of Taylor in Loup County in 1918. She's lived her entire life in the Sand Hills, and some ninety years later, she still remembers with awe standing at her mother's side as she made school lunches in the mornings for her and her siblings. "My mother would say, 'Isla, put on the teakettle.' I'd get the water hot, and I can just see her do it—she'd take a few crumbs of bread and drop it down to the chicken, grab it by the head and, this probably sounds gross to you, but she'd wring that chicken's head off." (The expression "wring your neck" has roots here, in farm food.)

By that time, the water was hot, and her mother would scald and pluck the chicken outside. "She'd bring it in the house, run a lot of cold water on it and cut it up into parts and fry it." When it was done, she put it into Isla's lunch pail along with an apple and a warning to keep the lid off the lunch pail because the chicken was still hot. Off they went to school, with a favorite lunch the family was lucky to have the resources to be able to eat. Fried chicken is still one of Isla's favorite meals, served with garden-picked vegetables like string beans. "I wished they'd had a chicken dressing contest," Isla recalls. "She'd have won it every time." Making lunches for school has certainly changed throughout the decades.

DRESSING A CHICKEN

At least once in your lifetime, if you eat chicken, you should participate in the full process of getting one to the dinner plate. To butcher a chicken, you must chop its head off or, as Isla remembers, wring its neck. The bird will flap around, sans head, and it's best to let it bleed out, upside down.

Rosie Murphy, also born and raised in the Sand Hills, has a great system set up for dressing chickens: two tree stumps, one with two nails driven into it and the other, hollowed out, about two feet from the "butchering block." She invited me over one afternoon to dress a few chickens with her—my first time killing an animal with my own hands to eat it. When butchering with this method, the chicken's head is placed between the two nails, exposing its neck while keeping the head in a fixed place. A very sharp and heavy hatchet is used to quickly sever the head from the body in one stroke. Immediately afterward, while still holding the feet, the chicken is held upside down inside the hollowed-out tree stump, allowing it to flap (as it will do for a good twenty seconds) and bleed out inside the tree stump. After the chicken quits moving, it must be scalded in hot water to loosen the feathers. After a few quick dips, pick the skin as clean as possible, reaching the small pin feathers if possible. Depending on the age of the bird, the skin is seared over a direct flame, which singes off the hair and any remaining feathers. Rinse the bird thoroughly, and at this point, it's ready to go inside.

To begin the process of "dressing" the bird, it needs another very thorough scrub to remove any remaining burned ends of pin feathers and hair. Then the skin must be removed from the neck to expose the entrance to the body cavity. Here, one must gently poke into the interior cavity, pulling skin away to

Rosie and Murph's butchering block, where chickens become dinner. I have eaten a lot of chicken in my life, and this was the first time I dressed one myself.

expose the "craw" or crop. Chances are it will be full of undigested grain. Very carefully pull the craw out as far as possible and slice it off with the grain still inside. Botching this will spill undigested grain all over the counter and inside the chicken cavity. Next the oil gland at the base of the bird must be removed. This gland produces oil that keeps the skin and feathers moisturized and will produce a bitter, oily flavor if cooked.

Then the intestines and interior organs must be removed. This also must happen carefully, as you do not want to rupture the intestine, which contains bacteria in the fecal matter. Slicing around the bottom of the bird, you must make an opening through the skin large enough to be able to reach in and pull out the organs. They should come out in one handful. After this, you can butterfly the chicken to get inside to remove the lungs, heart and egg sac matter. Experienced chicken dressers will reach inside the cavity and do this without beginning to part out the bird. Remove the neck, gizzard and heart and save those for stock. Rosie buries the remaining contents or feeds them to barn cats.

Now the chicken is ready for a straightforward roasting or parting into eight parts and cooked. If you part the chicken, save the spine and neck for stock. For stock, you should have wing ends, gizzard, heart, neck and back if you butterfly the chicken. It's a labor-intensive task, and smelly, and a first-timer (like me) will take about forty-five minutes to part a bird. It seems Isla's mother could do the whole thing, including frying it and making the rest of a school lunch in this time—a true pioneer.

A CULINARY HISTORY OF THE NEBRASKA SAND HILLS

We've been told that beef is what's for dinner, but on many working ranches, chicken was—and still is—far more popular on kitchen tables. Easy to raise, breed and butcher, chickens could remain alive until needed for a meal, eliminating the need for proper food storage methods. Chickens (and turkeys) are also relatively easy to keep, and chicks could be purchased more easily once the rails brought provisions. Like hogs, they are inexpensive to feed since they eat "leftovers" from the house—scraps of vegetables and bread mixed in with a steady diet of grains. Chickens forage for bugs and worms in their natural environment as they hunt and peck, making their eggs and meat richer than without these additions to their diet. From start to finish, butchering and dressing can take less than an hour, and one young, four-pound chicken can feed six people as a main dish.

ISLA'S FRIED CHICKEN

When I first started speaking with people about what they ate growing up in the Sand Hills, there was no dish I heard more often than fried chicken and garden vegetables. Not only was it a very common meal, it was, and still is, a beloved one. Going out to pick vegetables from the garden for supper, as well as the smell of frying chicken filling the house, are common fond memories of the old days of farm and ranch life. This meal appears to be as typical before refrigeration and electricity as after since nothing for the meal needed to be refrigerated, and it was an amount of food that would feed an entire family without leftovers. Today, the chicken on dining tables might not be one freshly dressed, parted and fried, like Isla's mother's, but the vegetables might still be from the garden. By many recollections, this is still a favorite meal of many Sand Hills residents.

The unsung ingredient in this dish might surprise you: a large cast-iron skillet, with helper handle and lid, is essential to keeping it simple and consistent. For this recipe, enough lard is melted to create a one-inch-deep bath so the chicken parts are only partially submerged. The cast iron distributes the heat evenly and holds it, and as with almost everything in Sand Hills kitchens, the lid has multiple functions—it contains grease splatters and captures heat, which helps the top of the chicken cook while the bottom half is frying in the oil. I developed this recipe with Isla's story of her mother's fried chicken in mind.

SOME NOTES ON THE RECIPE: What our predecessors didn't have to help this recipe along was an instant-read meat thermometer. I use one in this recipe to check the meat for safe internal temperatures since we have more concern about bacterial contamination in today's chickens than in the past.

Since one twelve-inch skillet (any bigger and it's too big to move easily) is not large enough to fry a whole parted chicken, the parts are divided into two batches: dark meat legs and thighs and white meat wings and breasts, the latter of which have a slightly shorter cook time.

I used a combination of lard and vegetable oil. The lard adds an additional "meaty" flavor, but I found frying entirely in lard overpowers the chicken. I split the difference. You may use entirely one or the other based on what's available.

....

Serves: 6

SPECIAL EQUIPMENT
12-inch cast-iron skillet with helper handle and lid
digital kitchen thermometer
cooling rack

INGREDIENTS
2 cups heavy cream
2 tablespoons lemon juice
1 4- to 5-pound fresh, unfrozen young chicken for frying, parted,
    fat trimmed, skin on
1 tablespoon salt plus more for sprinkling on chicken
2 cups lard
2 cups vegetable oil
1½ cups flour
1 teaspoon cracked black pepper

METHOD
In a small bowl, add two cups of heavy cream and two tablespoons of lemon juice to sour it. Let stand for a half an hour (See Soured Cream recipe on page 92).

Part a whole chicken into legs, thighs, wings and deboned breasts. (Save the rest of the bird to make stock.) Turn the breasts skin side down and cut each breast straight down the middle, making four equally sized parts. Trim any fatty areas from all the parts and leave the skin on. This helps the coating adhere. Season each piece with a sprinkle of salt. Place the soured cream and the chicken into a 1-gallon heavy-duty plastic bag, seal and massage the cream around the parts. Leave this on the counter in a large bowl or a rimmed cookie sheet to catch any leaks. Let this marinate for 2 hours on the counter, which is the time the chicken needs to fully come up to room temperature.

Once the chicken is at room temperature, begin melting lard and vegetable oil in the skillet over medium heat and bring to 325°F when checked with a digital thermometer.

Place flour, salt and pepper in a large bowl, enough to contain a few pieces of chicken at a time. Remove pieces one at a time from the bag, let marinade drip off and place in the flour, turning to coat every surface of each piece. Repeat this with all four pieces of dark meat, placing each one carefully with tongs so the meat lands away from you into the oil. Once all four pieces are in, cover the skillet with a lid and leave alone for 6 minutes. Check chicken pieces and turn for another 6 minutes. You should see a deep golden brown crust when you turn the pieces. After 11 minutes, insert a meat thermometer into the thickest part of the drumstick and check to make sure it reads 165°F. If not, cover and check again in 2-minute intervals until 165°F is reached. When it does, remove the pieces to a cooling rack on a rimmed cookie sheet to catch the drippings. This method (as opposed to putting them on a paper towel–lined plate) prevents the chicken from getting soggy while it's waiting to be eaten. Place this rack in an oven on the lowest setting to keep the chicken warm.

Repeat the coating process with the white meat and wings and place into the oil for 5 minutes, covered. Turn and cover for another 5 minutes. Check the thickest piece after ten minutes for 165°F, covering at 2-minute intervals until temperature is reached. Remove these to the cookie sheet and serve to the table.

....

SKILLET STRING BEANS

Serves: 6

INGREDIENTS

1 pound fresh string beans, ends trimmed

2 tablespoons water

1 tablespoon bacon grease or canola oil

½ teaspoon salt or to taste

1 tablespoon butter

METHOD

Preheat a 12-inch heavy-bottomed stainless or cast-iron skillet to medium-high heat, about two minutes. When the pan is hot, add string beans. They should sizzle and pop when they hit the pan. Add water and immediately cover with a lid for 2 minutes to allow the beans to steam. After 2 minutes, remove lid and stir beans. When water has evaporated, add bacon grease (or oil) and salt. Stirring regularly, sauté for another 5 minutes or until beans are bright green through the center and have slight browning from sautéing. Stir in butter and, when melted, remove from pan to serving dish. Serve immediately.

SCHOOL LUNCHES

Sandhillers know you're not from these parts if you call lunch "lunch" and supper "dinner." People here call the noon meal "dinner" and the evening meal "supper." The only place where the word "lunch" means "lunch" in the Sand Hills is at school. Whatever you call it, lunch, or "dinner," used to be the largest meal of the day, making school lunches very important parts of meal-making on the farm for both the parents and the children. They needed to be portable, large, reheatable in winter and indestructible in summer.

Signs of struggle showed in the quality, or the amount, of the school lunch. Not all children were blessed with full lunch pails. Stories of hard times are common. Children brought pieces of bread with lard spread on them. Others had only raw potatoes that the schoolteacher would put on the top of the schoolroom stove to bake during class. She or he would turn them throughout the morning so they had the chance to cook all the way through before lunch. Eggs were free and plentiful since most ranchers owned chickens, but children were teased for the smell of egg sandwiches in a closed schoolroom. Soups and stews were easy to stretch for large families, so oftentimes children would bring soup poured directly into their lunch pails—in winter, it would be frozen solid by the time they got to school. The teacher would place the pails on the stove, and the soup would be hot by lunchtime. The presence of meat in a lunch pail was a sign, if not of ranch prosperity then at least a successful pantry and kitchen planning.

Stews have been used since the beginning of cooking to stretch ingredients into a meal that would feed everyone. Countless cultures have some soup or stew as a classic representation of a hearty, simple meal, from French bouillabaisse to Hungarian goulash. There is no disputing their adaptability and popularity. In the Sand Hills, if one early stew emerged, perhaps the most quintessential one is none other than chicken and noodles.

Chickens have specific ages at which they are best used in certain ways. Young birds under four months old are great for roasting. Older chickens up to nine months old can be fried. Anything older would likely be butchered and used as stewing hens, as their meat is tough, lean and gristly. They might not be ideal, but they were always used, especially since meat has always been the most expensive ingredient in the pantry. Because of this, recipes adapted around these tough birds. Boiling meat tenderizes it, and a two- or three-year-old hen must be boiled to be edible; the meat is shredded and returned to the pot to boil some more, perhaps into a stew or chicken and noodles. The hens that Rosie and I dressed were "multiple-hour boilers," which is to say, a couple of really old birds. I made the following stew out of one of them for Rosie and Murph as a thank-you for teaching me how to dress birds.

SAND HILLS STEW (CHICKEN AND NOODLES)

Chicken and noodles—a flavorful, brothy noodle stew—is eaten everywhere in the United States, and the Sand Hills is no exception. It makes a hearty, carb-rich meal, perfect for filling hungry bellies of hardworking family and ranch hands. Egg noodles are easy to make and require only four ingredients. The utility of stews shines in the ingredients list, as the measurements do not need to be exact. If you're low on carrots, add a parsnip to replace them. The results will be equally as delicious as the original recipe. This recipe is developed to make your own broth from a fresh chicken, which you will need to boil for the stew.

....

Serves: 8

INGREDIENTS

1 4-pound chicken, cleaned and parted

2 medium onions, halved

4 cloves of garlic, peeled

4 carrots, scrubbed, peeled, ends removed

4 parsnips, scrubbed, skin on, ends removed

1 tablespoon salt, plus any to taste

¼ teaspoon pepper plus any to taste

1 bay leaf

2 tablespoons olive oil, bacon grease or lard

2 ribs celery, chopped ½-inch thick

1 tablespoon each fresh thyme, sage, rosemary; or 1 tablespoon
    dried "Herbs de Provence"

1 batch egg noodles (see recipe on page 94) or about ½ pound dried

Method

For the stock: In a stockpot, add all the chicken parts, one onion chopped into quarters, four cloves of garlic, two whole carrots, two whole parsnips, a tablespoon of salt, pepper and the bay leaf to the pot. Fill the pot with water just until all the chicken parts are covered and bring to a simmer on medium-low heat. Check the pot in about 45 minutes to skim any foam or scum that surfaces. After 1½ hours, remove the chicken parts with tongs to a plate and let cool. Shred the meat from the bone either with two forks or by hand, removing the skin and bones to return to the pot to continue simmering. Cover the chicken meat so it doesn't dry out and let the stock simmer again while you are preparing the ingredients for stew.

For the stew: Slice remaining carrots and parsnips into ½-inch rounds. Halve the onion and slice ¼-inch thick. In a separate heavy-bottomed stew pot, heat olive oil or lard over medium heat; add carrots, parsnips, celery and onions; and sauté until the onions turn translucent and soften, about 10 minutes. Add herbs, salt, pepper and chicken meat and sauté together until herbs smell fragrant. Using a strainer to catch bones and vegetables from the stock, pour six cups of the simmering stock into this pot, reserving extra stock for adjustments later. Let this pot simmer, partially covered, for 1.5 hours, or until the liquid has reduced by about 25 percent. Taste to adjust flavor, adding more salt or pepper at this stage if necessary.

Finally, 30 minutes before serving, add in one batch of egg noodles and simmer until cooked through, about 20 minutes. If you desire a thicker stew at this stage, sift flour 1 tablespoon at a time into the pot and stir to thicken.

Serve in bowls with fresh biscuits and a leafy garden salad on the side.

Bread: The Sand Hills' First Social Media

Chicken, the favored protein on the plate, had a very important companion. Bread still reigns supreme over Sand Hills ranch kitchen tables. In early pioneer history, before yeast cakes or packets were readily available, yeast cultures were kept active by regularly feeding a liquid "starter" with water, flour and occasionally sugar. To start them, ranch wives needed a hospitable environment to attract wild yeast from the air. They created it by mixing a few ounces of potato water with a few tablespoons of flour and sugar to create a slurry. When left loosely covered with cloth overnight and kept warm, airborne wild yeast fed off the slurry and multiplied in the environment to make an active starter. This is also known as a sourdough starter and requires constant maintenance once active. The process can take days to make the starter active enough to use for leavening breads.

The women in Sand Hills' kitchens didn't invent "friendship bread," but they certainly perfected the use of it in the ranch days between the 1900s and the 1920s. Originally attributed in the United States to Amish colonies (and certainly the idea has perpetuated as long as leavened bread has been made), a friendship bread was starter cultivated in one ranch kitchen and would then be split off and given to a few women to multiply and maintain in their own kitchens. Baking was happening regularly in almost every ranch kitchen, so if someone lost their starter from lack of feeding it, extreme heat or cold, a neighboring ranch wife could give a cup from their own batch to the yeastless neighbor. It could take a week of careful cultivation to get a starter active and going from scratch, and travel to town or the money for store-bought yeast cake may not have been options. Ranch wives couldn't miss a baking day, or there would be no bread on the tables, so friendship bread, in this way, was as much a safety net as it was a social medium. It offered an occasion to travel off the ranches and visit with other ranch wives and provided a sense of community and connectedness in the isolated Sand Hills. In an era where there was very little actual money changing hands, cultivating something useful out of the air for free was far more fulfilling and consistent with ranch values than paying for it at a store.

Maintaining a yeast culture involves "feeding" it every day if kept at room temperature or every few days if kept in the refrigerator. To feed, one stirs the flour and water mixture (usually a quart or so) and discards one-half cup of it. Then the starter is replenished with one-half cup of water and one-fourth cup flour. The "discard" is only to help keep the mixture fresh and can still be used in baking. When using larger amounts for baking, at least one cup of original starter is left in the container, and the amount removed is the amount of water and flour replaced at roughly a 2:1 ratio to bring the culture back up to the original amount. I made and maintained a two-quart starter while testing found bread recipes, and it is enough to bake seven or eight loaves in one batch.

Bread was so important to ranch tables that baking it had its own day on the chore list. Starters were in heavy use in early ranch times, when single baking days generated eight to ten loaves of bread for the week. Many Sand Hills recipes can, and usually do, serve more than one purpose, offer more than one substitution or solve more than one problem. Bread recipes found in personal collections and old Sand Hills cookbooks are perfect examples. Many were master recipes—the week's bread, rolls and sweet pastry were made at the same time from the same batch of dough. I uncovered a "Dutch Cake" recipe in a Cherry County family history entitled "Only Yesterday" that unlocked a story about baking day. The recipe begins the night before with a recipe for a yeast starter accelerated by cake yeast, created from a half cake of yeast and potato water. From this, a large, basic soft dough recipe was made and left to rise. From it, bread loaves, rolls and cinnamon rolls (or

"Dutch Cake") were made, usually all on the same day. It is a very typical Sand Hills recipe—sturdy and delicate, just like the Sand Hills themselves.

Yeast thrives in a cultured environment and can live indefinitely as long as it has food (flour) and water to nourish it. San Francisco, known for its sourdough bread bakeries, claims to have strains kept alive for one hundred years or more. Many Sand Hills ranch women recall working with starters, but they also recall them being the first ingredient to be replaced with reliable, no-maintenance yeast cakes or packets as soon as the opportunity and money made themselves available. Piecing together a timeline of the change from yeast starters to store-bought yeast is a bit of a challenge. As cookbooks in the region tell it, starters seem to have died out in the 1930s, although they enjoyed a modest popular resurgence in the 1960s.

One thing is for certain: maintaining a starter in a remote Sand Hills ranch kitchen was a necessity if there was no way to purchase yeast. The process of starting a yeast culture is almost the same everywhere, but the description for maintaining one in "Only Yesterday" reflected the author's mother's instructions to keep the starter "as warm as a baby." There is no better description. If the average room temperature is somewhere between sixty-eight and seventy-two degrees, "as warm as a baby" is warmer, in the seventy-five- to eighty-degree range. Many women kept their starters on a shelf near the stove for this reason. Maintaining a starter is a fussy prospect, but what you spend in effort is returned in flavor in the breads made from it. Once a yeast culture is started and active, it can be used to leaven any bread from savory to sweet pastry.

• •

YEAST STARTER

INGREDIENTS
2 quarts water, plus more to replace evaporation
1 small potato, peeled and rinsed
½ cup sugar
1½ active dry yeast packets

METHOD
In two quarts of water, boil the potato for about 20 minutes or until completely soft. With a fork, mash it until it dissolves in the

Left: If you stay
on the interstate
in Nebraska,
this is the only
landscape you
will see.

Below: I know
they're docile, but
cows are still very
large animals to
stare you down. I
let him pass.

Keith Colburn bottle-feeds each of the piglets getting "shorted," a term for those unable to push through the rest of the litter to reach their mother's milk. He raises about 150 hogs per year in a free-range environment.

The Spade Ranch cook would ring the bell on the side of the cookhouse to signal when meals were ready. Today, it remains as a relic of a past era. *Courtesy of Clay Bixby.*

Sand Hills–style address book—just keep a close watch on your odometer. No Google Maps app necessary, or available, in these remote parts of the hills.

Irrigation methods allow for more grass to be grown on the Sand Hills. These hayfields have just been mowed and bailed.

Cattle grazing on the Sand Hills.

Rolling Sand Hills in Cherry County. In the distance, a "blowout," a patch of exposed, bare sand, scars the hill. Blowouts are difficult to control once started and can be caused by anything from excessive rainfall to burrowing animals or overgrazing.

A Sand Hills sunset.

Old meets new in wind-powered energy in Custer County. New wind turbines create clean energy for the electrical grid, while an old windmill provides water for a herd of cattle.

Apples placed in the skillet for the upside-down apple tart, with wild plum jelly in the background.

Apple tart out of the oven, waiting to be flipped.

Apple tart, successfully flipped onto a plate.

Fresh biscuits and strawberry-rhubarb jam. Very early recipes for biscuits and cornbread were made on the stovetop, usually in cast-iron skillets.

I tested the Master Sand Hills Biscuit recipe with both lard and butter as the fat. The verdict? Butter is better.

Baking day typically included many different variations of baked goods. Rolls, loaves and sweets were all crafted from the same batch of dough.

"Dutch cake." It is not the most attractive pastry, but it is deliciously gooey, sweet and decadent when served warm. It is a sweet pastry made from the same bread dough as the rolls and loaves. This can also be rolled, cut into slices and laid spiral side up to bake like cinnamon rolls.

Simple, satisfying egg noodles, separated and drying before going into Chicken and Noodles.

Isla's Fried Chicken. I developed this recipe after sitting down with Isla Emerton and hearing her recount her favorite meal. It was a common farm and ranch dinner that is still a favorite today, but it is not made as often as it once was.

I showed Eldora Muirhead this photo I took of my Uncle Bob's breakfast ingredients as he was trying to make breakfast for me and my Aunt Karen in Valentine, and she said, "Those stand up well." It's a compliment; fresh farm eggs should have deep orange yolks that stand very high from the whites.

Fresh green beans, picked right from the garden, cooked and sent right to the table, are a ranch kitchen favorite.

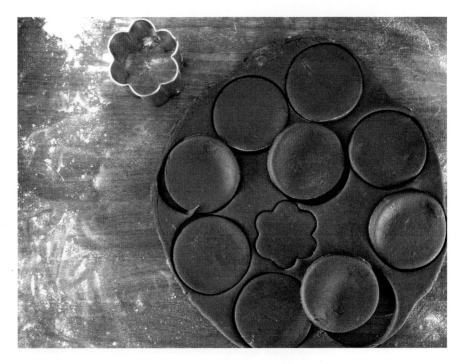

Rolling out Grandma Hoefs's Molasses Cookies. The smaller cookie cutter is to squeeze an extra cookie out of a section before rerolling. You'll try anything after realizing you need to roll about one hundred more cookies.

The key to a great pot roast is to buy the best cut of meat you can afford. Pot roasts were very commonly made when large batches of food were needed on Sand Hills ranches, and while it may be expensive, there is no shortage of fantastic beef.

Making fresh fruit shortcakes with soured whipped cream. Use any fruits you like in this recipe. In early summer, this could be a strawberry shortcake. Mid- to late summer brings peaches and raspberries.

I found some! A gallon jar of raw milk was delivered to my place in Burwell. I left a "donation" to the cow that provided it to me.

Jim Raye, a Valley County resident, shows me his haul of native wild plums harvested from his pastures. I followed him to his friend's house, where he traded the bucket of plums for a few jars of homemade wild plum jelly. He gave me one of the jars, which I later used to make the upside-down apple tart.

Eldora's Lemon Cake—a modest update to an original recipe recollected by Eldora Muirhead.

Biscuits become dessert when made into short cakes. While any fresh fruit will do, the classic topping is strawberry.

Ingredients for Uncle Gus's Fish Hash. Starting with fresh-caught fish and good farm eggs is essential to this simple dish.

Chicken and Noodles—a staple dish made entirely from scratch with ingredients from the garden and chicken coop.

Resurrecting fish for breakfast in a fish hash. In early Sand Hills days, fish was served at the first meal after it was caught. With fishing best before dawn and after dusk, that next meal was usually breakfast.

A wheelbarrow full of pie pumpkins, just picked from a garden.

water. You should have a cloudy liquid. Drain the remaining water into a liquid measure and replace the evaporated water to make 2 quarts. Place this into a 1-gallon glass jar. When the water cools to warm, between 75 and 90°F, add ½ cup of sugar and 1½ packets of yeast. Store this in the warmest part of the house overnight, loosely covering the opening with a clean cloth. In 24 hours, you should have a bubbling, frothy mixture that smells of both yeast and alcohol.

Starting from scratch (no yeast packet) is tricky business, since the environment you're creating is equally as hospitable to bacteria as it is to yeast. I found it easiest to start with a yeast packet and leave the slurry covered with a canvas towel on the counter to continue to attract wild yeast from the air. Once any yeast, wild or packaged, takes hold, the environment becomes inhospitable to bacteria, and your task is to keep the yeast culture fed, fresh and happy. When using a lid to store, keep it loose, as yeast produces gasses that can build pressure in an airtight container. If stored in the refrigerator, this can happen every three or four days. If "kept warm as a baby" on the kitchen counter, it will need to be fed every 12 hours. Adding this feeding to the chore list on the farm or ranch wasn't as much of a task as it is in today's world.

As the starter becomes less active, a thin, alcoholic-scented liquid will separate and rise to the top. This liquid is called the "hooch," and you can stir it back into the starter. To maintain the starter, stir it well and then remove a ½ cup of starter (or more, if you're baking with it). For every ½ cup of starter removed, feed the starter with ¼ cup of flour and ½ cup of tepid water and stir thoroughly. If you maintain about a quart, you'll easily have enough for a few loaves of bread any time you bake. This recipe is for 2 quarts, about 1 quart of which you'll use to bake the following bread recipe two days later. You can then maintain 1 quart of starter—a more manageable amount.

· ·

MASTER RECIPE: BREAD

This recipe makes four loaves of bread, or three loaves plus a Dutch Cake.

INGREDIENTS
¼ cup sugar
2 teaspoons salt
7 cups flour, plus about 1 cup for adjusting the recipe and flouring the board
¼ cup butter (or lard)
3½ cups liquid starter (see recipe on page 64)
2 teaspoons olive or vegetable oil

METHOD
Sift all dry ingredients into a very large bowl. With your hands, cut in butter until fully blended into the flour. Make a well for the liquid and add starter. Gently mix ingredients together with a wooden spoon to form a dough. You might need to add up to another cup of flour in order to keep the dough from sticking to your hands. When dough comes together in a ball, knead for a few minutes by hand to make sure the dough is well mixed. Lightly oil a large bowl and the dough, place in the bowl and cover with a towel. Let dough rest until it has doubled in size, about 2 hours in a warm area. When the dough has doubled in size, punch it down and split into four equal quarters.

For loaves: Knead quarters for about 2 minutes each into oblong shapes. Place into oiled 9x5-inch loaf pans, oil the tops and let rise uncovered in a cold oven until the tops of the loaves pass the top of the loaf pan, about 2 hours. Brush tops with cream and bake at 350°F for 55 minutes, rotating once at 30 minutes.

For rolls: Pinch palm-sized amounts from the dough and knead about 1 minute each into rolls. Place the rolls, barely touching, in an oiled 8x8-inch cake pan. Oil the tops and let rise in a cold oven until the tops pass the top of the pan or they have doubled in size, about 2 hours. Brush tops with cream and bake at 350°F for 40 minutes.

For Dutch Cake: Roll dough to fit into a 9x14-inch baking dish. Place in oiled baking dish and let double in size, about 2 hours. See the following recipe.

DUTCH CAKE

"The Dutch cake was made by taking a generous pinch of dough and flattening it out in a glass baking dish. It was then allowed to rise in a warm place until doubled in size, and covered with a mixture of one cup heavy, slightly sour cream blended with a cup of sugar, a teaspoon of vanilla, and a sprinkle of cinnamon over the top. This was baked until the top was well browned and bubbly and served in squares, hot from the oven."

The inspiration for this recipe is also taken from "Only Yesterday." In it, the author described the Dutch Cake as a sweet pastry "for the apprentice baker." The more accomplished baker could have taken the same topping, spread it on the unrisen dough, rolled it, cut it into individual rolls and set those in the pan to rise before baking. This technique is what was used to make cinnamon rolls on baking day, perhaps with the addition of sugar icing.

Many Sand Hills women recount a version of yeasted bread dough sweetened into a cake and baked in a baking dish. Some call it a German Cake, others a Dutch Cake. Whatever the name, it was an easy, sweet treat made from a section of dough that could also be shaped into a loaf of bread. The previous dough recipe will also make all the other breads in this book, plus the Dutch Cake—highlighting both how simple and how similar Sand Hills cooking is across cultures. Eldora remembers a similar cake that she would make as a "cake that looked ugly but tasted great." Indeed it does.

••

Serves 8–10

INGREDIENTS
1 quarter of master bread dough (see recipe on page 66)

Toppings for Dutch Cake
1 cup heavy, soured cream (see recipe on page 92)
1 cup sugar
1 teaspoon vanilla
2 teaspoons cinnamon, plus a sprinkling for the top

METHOD

For the topping: In a small bowl, mix topping ingredients together. Cover with plastic wrap and place in the refrigerator until use.

For the dough: Roll dough to fit into a 9x14-inch baking dish. Place in oiled baking dish and let double in size, about 2 hours.

Assembly: Preheat oven to 350°F. Using your fingertips, poke depressions in the dough about an inch apart, to allow the topping to pool in them. Spread the topping mixture evenly over the cake. Place baking dish on center rack and bake for 35–40 minutes, until the top is golden and bubbling brown.

Note: You may also make this cake with premade bread or pizza dough from the refrigerated aisle in the grocery store.

Since nothing goes to waste in the Sand Hills, recipes appeared in cookbooks using that discarded cup of starter, including sourdough pancakes and a unique recipe found in Cherry County for sourdough cookies called "Grubstake Cookies." It makes a sponge from half a cup of starter by adding flour and sugar, letting it rise and then adding in eggs, more flour, cocoa powder and brown sugar.

SOURDOUGH PANCAKES

This recipe is an adaptation of a number of sourdough recipes found in cookbooks across the Sand Hills and is a great use of the starter typically discarded every day. It makes delicious, tangy pancakes. Since not many people keep starters these days, this recipe has a buttermilk adaptation at the end.

....

Serves: 4

INGREDIENTS
1½ cups starter, room temperature
½ cup milk
1½–2 cups flour
2 eggs
2 tablespoons sugar

Combine ingredients together, reserving ½ cup of flour to adjust consistency of batter (if a thicker batter is desired.) Once combined, let sit for 30 minutes at warm room temperature until you see bubbles of activity at the top of the batter. Then gently add the following and mix thoroughly:

2 teaspoons baking powder
4 tablespoons melted butter, plus 2 tablespoons melted butter for brushing tops of pancakes
1 teaspoon pure vanilla extract
1 teaspoon salt
zest of one lemon (optional)

METHOD
Let mixture rest for another 15 minutes, until it appears to stiffen in the container. Preheat a 12-inch skillet on medium heat and oil when hot. Pour batter into 4-inch pancakes. The pancake should start rising immediately and lightly brown around the edges in about 2 minutes. Let the bubbles on the top of the pancake begin to slow before flipping, and cook for another 2 minutes, or until the second side is golden brown. Adjust heat up or down depending on the desired color of the pancake—a medium golden brown is best. Oil the pan in between batches.

Brush remaining melted butter on the tops of each pancake, stack into the center of plates and top with desired toppings (chopped walnuts or pecans, fresh blueberries, banana slices or fresh whipped cream) and real maple syrup.

BUTTERMILK PANCAKE VERSION: *Use 2 cups buttermilk in place of the starter and milk. In this version, increase the baking powder to 1 tablespoon and do not rest the batter. Mix it up and make some buttermilk pancakes!*

Biscuits and cornbread are popular recipes found in Sand Hills cookbooks. Cornbread at one point was so popular that Everett Dick called it "eternal cornbread" in *The Sod-House Frontier*. Quick breads provided the baker with short-term solutions to more time-consuming leavened bread. They can get to the table in an hour or less, perhaps out of necessity if yeasted recipes failed. Biscuits were so commonly made that recipes were almost unnecessary; many women could tell me a recipe by heart. Church, extension and social club cookbooks are flooded with solid biscuit recipes, and quite often "master" biscuit mixes were kept or printed—large-batch mixes that could be made once and would make four or five batches. No special equipment was needed. For every recipe that uses a biscuit cutter to cut biscuits into rounds, there is a recipe that calls for a juice glass to cut biscuits or a knife to cut into squares.

References to the first biscuits original settlers made appear in cookbooks and family histories as "hardtack"—crude, edible biscuits containing only flour and water and baked until they held together. When sod houses and their modest kitchens were built from the 1850s forward, there was usually enough money to add a leavener, baking powder, to the pantry. Cream surfaced around the same time in recipes, and biscuits made a significant leap forward in flavor and texture. "Cream biscuits" weren't as tough as hardtack, and with few as four ingredients—flour, cream, baking powder and salt—they became common in kitchens since they could be made every day with little preparation.

In the 1920s, when kitchens were fully established and hogs were regularly raised and butchered, lard made appearances into biscuit recipes as a fat to separate flour from water during baking. This separation adds flakiness and height. The biscuit's final evolution in cookbooks seems to be replacing the lard with butter, a more favored fat that gives biscuits a lighter flavor than lard. It's hard to say if it's coincidence that cornbread recipes began disappearing from cookbooks at about the same time as the cream biscuit appeared, but the two do share at least one thing in common: they were the first things made if the household ran out of yeast for bread.

The biscuits here were also tested with raw milk to replicate the kind ranch wives baked pre-1960s, before milk pasteurization became common in the Sand

Hills. Just like using raw milk or pasteurized in Eldora's cake recipe, the original biscuit recipe tested with raw milk yielded a fuller flavor and richer texture, if a little dense. (The mantra "fat is flavor" in kitchens everywhere is true!) I can't say it enough: if you have the opportunity to bake with raw milk, do it! The following master biscuit recipe reflects an updated recipe for pasteurized milk. If you do use raw milk, add an extra tablespoon to the recipe here.

As for the fats in the recipe, I tested the biscuits with lard and again with butter. Lard works very well to create a flaky biscuit but produces a vaguely meaty aroma to the biscuits, which is fine if you're serving them with a meat dish, but if you are serving the biscuits as a short cake for dessert (see the Sand Hills Short Cake recipe afterward), you won't want the meaty flavor near a sweet treat.

A round, sharp biscuit cutter makes traditional biscuits that tend to rise evenly. I use a crinkle cutter for no other reason than I like the look it gives to the biscuit edges. In absence of a cutter, cutting the biscuits into squares with a knife was the next best technique (over using a juice glass) to get a good, even rise on the biscuits. In every case, they're all still equally delicious.

I was intrigued by a large-batch biscuit recipe in an old Custer County cookbook, compiled by the Home Demonstration Club and Home Extension Council, calling for the cook to measure out all the dries and mix and store them as needed for batches of biscuits. When biscuits were needed, a measure of mix and a measure of cream were the only recipe steps required for a batch of biscuits. It's a great shortcut that highlights the resourcefulness and efficiency of a Sand Hills kitchen, and I find myself making biscuits more often at home with my own mix stored and at the ready.

• •

MASTER BISCUIT MIX
Makes: 10–12 biscuits

INGREDIENTS
8 cups flour, sifted
¼ cup plus 1 teaspoon baking powder
1 tablespoon, plus 1 teaspoon salt

METHOD
Sift 8 cups of flour into a large bowl. Measure back 8 cups of flour (you should have about ½ cup left over; replace it into the flour

container to reuse later). Add baking powder and salt and mix thoroughly with a whisk. Portion 2 cups of mix into four zip-top plastic bags, reserving the leftover to use to flour the board when you make a batch. Label the bags "Biscuit Mix" and voila—you have four individual batches of biscuit mix awaiting use.

SAND HILLS BISCUITS (SINGLE BATCH)

Special Equipment
2½-inch round crinkle cutter or biscuit cutter
parchment paper

Ingredients
1 package "biscuit mix"
4 tablespoons chilled, cubed butter (or lard)
½ cup heavy cream
½ cup whole milk

Method
Preheat oven to 450°F. Add "biscuit mix" to bowl and then add butter, working through with your hands until the texture resembles Sand Hills earth (fine sand). Add cream and milk and mix just until combined. It will be sticky. Gently turn dough out onto a floured surface. Handling as little as possible, pat with floured hands or gently roll to ½ inch thick with a floured rolling pin. Cut rounds with a biscuit cutter and place each biscuit onto a cookie sheet covered in parchment paper.

Bake in the center of the oven for 12–14 minutes or until tops are golden brown, rotating once during baking. Optional: For cheese biscuits, mix in ¼ cup shredded cheddar cheese to mix and sprinkle tops with another ¼ cup cheese. Baking time remains the same.

DESSERTS

Desserts are the one course that have evolved dramatically in the last century on the Great Plains. One hundred years ago, a dessert might have been the Sand Hills Short Cakes—a simple alteration of a biscuit with fresh fruit and a scoop of cream on top. In the 1930s, a typical dessert might have been a sour cream pie. In the 1960s, perhaps the most common dessert was "heavenly hash," some combination of nondairy whipped topping, canned fruit and marshmallows. The biscuit recipe, like the bread recipe, shines in its adaptability.

....

SUMMER FRUIT SHORT CAKES
Serves: 10–12

The simple addition of sugar to the biscuit recipe makes them leap from supper sides to featured desserts. Add 3 tablespoons of sugar to one "biscuit mix" package, brush these biscuit tops with milk, sprinkle a little sugar on each top and you have a short cake.

INGREDIENTS
soured whipped cream (see recipe on page 92)

FRUIT TOPPING
1 pint raspberries
3 large, fresh peaches, skins on, pitted and thinly sliced lengthwise
¼ cup sugar
¼ cup lemon juice (about 2 lemons, plus zest for garnish, optional)
10–12 mint leaves (for garnish, optional)

BISCUITS
1 package "biscuit mix"
3 tablespoons sugar, plus 2 tablespoons extra for dusting tops
    OR 2 cups flour, sifted
1 tablespoon plus ¼ teaspoon baking powder
3 tablespoons sugar, plus 2 tablespoons extra for dusting tops
¾ teaspoon kosher salt
– –

¼ cup unsalted butter, chilled and cut into ¼-inch cubes
½ cup heavy cream
½ cup whole milk, plus 2 tablespoons extra for brushing tops

METHOD

For the fruit topping: Before starting biscuits, gently toss fruit, sugar and lemon juice in a large bowl. Place in the refrigerator, covered, for 20 minutes. The berries will give some juice and soften in this time.

For the biscuits: Preheat oven to 450°F. Line a sheet pan with parchment paper and set aside.

For biscuits from scratch: Sift 2 cups of flour into a large bowl. Measure out 2 cups of the sifted flour into a separate bowl. You will have some leftover flour from the air added in by sifting; use this for rolling the dough. Add baking powder, 3 tablespoons sugar and salt and mix until combined. If using biscuit mix: add one package to bowl, along with 3 tablespoons sugar.

Add butter, working through the mixture with your hands until the consistency resembles wet sand. Add cream and ½ cup milk and mix by hand just until the dough comes together, about 1 minute. (It should look uneven and barely hold together.)

On a floured surface, gently roll out the dough to ½ inch thickness. Cut the dough using a 2½-inch round cookie or biscuit cutter and place each disc on the parchment-lined sheet pan. Brush the tops with a little milk or cream, sprinkle with sugar (a heavy pinch per biscuit) and place on the cookie sheet. Roll the dough scraps once more to make two more biscuits. Bake for 6 minutes and then rotate the pan. Bake for another 4–5 minutes, for a total of 11 minutes, or until the tops are golden brown. Remove and let cool.

Halve the biscuits lengthwise and place two halves each on small dessert plates. Top each with a large spoonful of berries and then whipped cream. Finish each with a pinch of lemon zest and a mint leaf, if desired. If you'd like a sweeter dessert, sprinkle a little sugar on top. Serve immediately.

Another ingredient that holds a special place in Nebraska kitchens is the apple. Apple trees grow well in the southeastern part of the state, and the rest of the state enjoys the bounty of those crops. When considering developing a pie recipe, I kept coming back to my trusty 12-inch skillet, which was becoming my best friend in the kitchen. I didn't want to leave it out, so while sifting through hundreds of pie recipes, I decided to turn the idea on its head, literally. Inspired by common ingredients that flourish in Nebraska, I adapted a tarte tatin recipe, or an upside-down apple tart, baked in the same workhorse of a 12-inch skillet that chicken could be fried in. The apples are sautéed in a sugar and butter mixture in the skillet, a rolled-out pie dough is placed on top and the entire pan is put in the oven and baked. After it comes out of the oven, it's cooled, flipped and glazed with chokecherry or wild plum jam.

UPSIDE-DOWN APPLE TART
Makes one 12-inch tart

SPECIAL EQUIPMENT
12-inch cast-iron skillet
pastry brush

INGREDIENTS
1 cup sugar
½ cup butter (one stick)
pinch of salt
9–10 large, tart apples (such as Pink Lady, Braeburn, Honey Crisp or Granny Smith*), peeled, quartered and seeded into 36–40 quarters
1 premade pie dough, rolled to 12-inch diameter (or use your favorite homemade recipe)
¼ cup chokecherry, wild plum or sandcherry jam, or other tart jam or jelly
2 tablespoons water
1 teaspoon lemon juice

*If using Granny Smith apples, add an extra 2 tablespoons sugar to the recipe.

METHOD
Preheat oven to 350°F. Preheat skillet on medium-low heat. Place sugar, butter and a pinch of salt into skillet and let melt while prepping apples. Stir occasionally.

Place peeled and quartered apples stacked against one another, one cut side down in a circle following the outside rim of the pan. Fill in the middle section of pan with remaining apples (depending on the size of the apples, you might have a few quarters left over). Increase heat to medium and sauté the apples without touching them until you see the sugar begin to turn a light golden brown. Then, one by one, flip each apple to the other cut side, keeping them in place. When sugar mixture turns a medium golden brown and bubbles up between the apples (about 10 minutes), turn off the heat and add the pie dough to the top. Carefully tuck the dough in down between the edge of the pan and the apples to create a lip to keep any sauce inside the tart when it's flipped. In the middle of the dough, cut two small vents for steam to escape and place in the middle rack of the oven. Bake for 40–45 minutes or until the top of the dough is golden brown.

When done, remove from oven to a trivet and let cool for 10 minutes. Run a knife around the outside edge of the dough and invert a plate to cover the top of the pan. In one, slow action, with kitchen towels or oven mitts, flip the pan and plate, carefully setting the plate on the counter, pan on top. The tart should free itself from the pan and land on the plate intact. Scrape out any slices of apple that stuck to the pan and replace them on the tart.

Dilute jam with water and lemon juice and, using a pastry brush, brush the tart with the jam. Slice and serve with vanilla ice cream on the side.

BEEF

If bread was life, you'd think beef was king on the table in ranch country. Cows are everywhere in the Sand Hills, and beef is a valuable commodity on the larger U.S. and world market. It might be surprising to learn, then, that beef is not "what's for dinner" on many Sand Hills ranch tables.

Constructing a food history is as much about what people ate as what they did not. Irene Nelson Walker never ate beef. "We could never afford it. We had hogs, and the cellar was full of canned goods, but we never had beef." On a day in 1948, her mother brought some home, and Irene ate her first cut of red meat. She was eighteen years old. Red meat was very expensive and, if owned, would be sold for profit, she recalls. And without electricity on the ranch, they had no way to store the eight-hundred-plus pounds of meat that butchering one cow would provide. She describes growing up "poor but happy" and remembers, "We ate a lot of fried chicken." Poor or not, this was a very common meal on average-sized ranches. Her daughter, Tammy, who now runs 1+1 Ranch with her husband, Jerry, recalls the same popular supper. Today, they eat beef, but like her mother, she didn't grow up eating it. The beef they do eat today is from their own cattle, stored in a locker rented from the meat processor in town, twelve miles away. Very rarely do they buy meat at the store.

The impact of beef is felt in other ways. The quality and number of cattle here are legendary in the Great Plains, and there is no bigger producer of cattle per square mile in Nebraska than the Sand Hills. Cherry County, Nebraska's largest county, is also the largest beef-producing county in the *country*, according to the Nebraska Beef Council, raising 166,000 cows in 2012. Second to it is another county in the Sand Hills, Custer County, with 100,000. In Nebraska, Holt County is the third-largest beef-producing county in the nation (by the number of 99,000). As a state, cattle outnumber people four to one when you total the number of cows that are "finished" on feedlots in the state. In all, 6,150,000 cattle resided in Nebraska in 2013. In Cherry County, cows outnumber people by about thirty to one.

The Colburns are on their fifth generation raising cattle on the same land. We drive through herds of cattle across the ranch to see the site

A steak dinner has always been a special meal. This coupon is still handed out to regular customers today as a courtesy by the Burwell Livestock Market to redeem anywhere steak is served in Burwell. This is a true Sand Hills gesture—this coupon is honored graciously and without question.

of the old fish camp, where Delores points out one of the lakes on their ranch. There used to be floating islands in it when the lake was deeper—groups of rushes that would get pushed around by the prairie winds. They'd come out and watch them "because there's not much else to do out here." Another reason was that they love the land, and observing it is part of the ranch way of life. In a way, the ranch itself, and the other ranches around it that make up the largest cattle-producing county in the country, are all floating islands.

"Not much is new out here; we have old cars, and we fix everything ourselves." This far out, you have to. A service call costs mileage from Valentine, forty miles away, plus $50 to $100 per hour depending on what needs to be serviced. We were driving the narrow road back to the house after seeing the ranch's lakes when Delores reflected, "People think we're simple out here, living a ranch life." It's a statement acknowledging the stigma of rural life. For a moment, I thought about it. In a way, she's right. By now, running a one-hundred-year-old ranch should be simple. They've had generations of practice solving the problems that arise in this sort of business. It wasn't the kind of "simple" Delores was referring to, to be sure. Coca-Cola, Heinz and Campell's Soup also make and deliver a food product to an international market every year and have done so for more than a century, and you would be hard-pressed to find someone to call their operations simple. "I don't want to brag, but we're not servicing a bank with this life." I wonder if other centennial food companies, like Hershey or Hormel, can say the same.

The meat from butchering one cow is a huge amount for one family to store, even in modern times with large-capacity deep freezers in Sand Hills basements. Before reliable electrical refrigeration, this amount of meat was a near impossibility for one family to store using alternative preservation methods like searing and storing in hot fat, smoking or drying. Four families splitting one cow will still each need to prepare and store two hundred pounds of meat, a multi-day process for a cook to break down and properly slice, prepare and store, even with help. Many of the small meat processors that dot the Sand Hills have cold-storage lockers where people can keep their quantities of meat, accessing the lockers when they plan to eat some of their store. Like Tammy and Jerry Rowse, Delores and Dean keep meat from a cow they butcher annually in a meat locker in Valentine.

The larger the operation, the easier it was to eat beef. Beef as a regular meal on the tables tended to be reserved for large-scale ranches that employed multiple people and ranch families. On the historic Spade Ranch in the western Sand Hills, Stephanie Bixby Graham—the granddaughter of Lawrence Bixby, preserver of the well-known Spade Ranch—recalls "always" having roasts. However, they were always feeding at least fifteen people per day, enough hungry traffic to install a cookhouse on the ranch, with a full-time cook to manage it. Roasts were cooked "old-fashioned" style, in large roasting pans in the oven, and would feed many. Each roast was typically fifteen pounds or more. With that volume, it was easier to go through a side of beef without losing it to spoilage; on this scale, beef made sense to put on the table.

The Spade Ranch at one point in time enveloped seventy-five thousand acres and is now more than twenty-five thousand acres split among three surviving Bixby family members.

The Spade Ranch cookhouse fed family members, ranch hands, delivery people—"anyone who needed to make a delivery to the ranch, propane, bankers, feed salesmen, they always came at noon, because they knew they'd get a meal." And as Stephanie recalls, there was always enough food and an extra place setting. This was typical ranch hospitality. You'd never not feed a visitor, even if he were coming to collect a payment.

The cookhouse on the Spade Ranch. This log structure was moved from the Newman Ranch in 1888 to the Spade Ranch and used as the cookhouse until the 1970s. It is still standing today and occupied by descendants of Lawrence Bixby, "the Preserver of the Old Spade Ranch." *Courtesy Stephanie Bixby Graham.*

Jim Thayer, the Spade Ranch's first full-time cook, standing at the back of the chuck wagon, protected from the sun by a canvas tent, circa 1904. *Courtesy of Stephanie Bixby Graham.*

Although less so today, beef is still a special-occasion meat. Beef is expensive on the market, and choice cuts like rib-eye and prime rib sell for top dollar. I told Eldora that I was developing a pot roast recipe that calls for a four-pound cut of chuck roast, and she joked, "That's $100 of meat in that pot, isn't it?"

EASY POT ROAST

Almost every ranch kitchen has a collection of handwritten recipes for branding dinners. In ranch culture, brandings are one of the biggest social events of the year, typically long weekends filled with work, bonfires at night and a whole lot of eating. Ranch wives often serve the same food every branding, pulling out foolproof, large-batch recipes to fill the bellies of thirty-five to fifty hungry friends, neighbors and family members who help each ranch place marks on cattle to identify them between herds. Large cuts of beef and pork (usually hams) pop up in cookbooks and recipe boxes across the Sand Hills. Fifteen- to twenty-pound beef roasts bake for hours on large trays, along with full pans of potatoes. Crockpots of macaroni and cheese simmer on counters, fillings for fruit pies are made in tubs and held for baking in assembly-line batches and tabletop fryers come out to fry chickens. It's all served buffet style using any surface possible, and any ranch wife will tell you that it's best to keep the crowd outside. The men are dirty, and in the spring it's usually warm out; for everyone's sanity, *that* many hungry men should stay outside to eat.

This pot roast is made with only eight ingredients, including the salt and pepper! With so few ingredients, it is important to use the best available, especially the beef, the main ingredient. If you can find home-grown or grass-fed beef, this is the dish for it. How long has it been since you've replaced your pepper? This recipe is also a great reason to upgrade to a grinder full of fresh whole peppercorns. Combine those with some home-grown or farmers' market vegetables, and this dish shines. And as with any Sand Hills recipe, it's highly adaptable. If you don't have two pounds of potatoes, add a few parsnips to make up the difference. If you have some leftover beef or chicken broth, or a little extra red or white wine, use it as the liquid measure in the recipe. That will only add more flavor to the dish.

Today, dishes like these can be made in crockpots. In fact, many stories of brandings include recollections of "crockpot brigades," but I suggest using a Dutch oven that travels from stove top to oven.

· ·

Serves: 6—8

INGREDIENTS

3½- to 4-pound cut chuck roast

1 tablespoon salt

1 teaspoon pepper

2 tablespoons vegetable or canola oil, or bacon grease

1 large white or yellow onion, sliced into ½-inch-thick rounds and halved

6 medium carrots, scrubbed, skin on

2—2½ pounds baby or small potatoes (halved if large, whole if baby)

½ cup water

¼ cup flour

METHOD

Preheat oven to 300°F. Preheat heavy Dutch oven on medium-high heat on a burner. On a separate work area, rinse and pat dry the chuck roast. Heavily salt and pepper each side.

In Dutch oven, add oil and let heat. When it is shimmering, add the pot roast and sear each side for 2—3 minutes or until a light golden crust forms. Remove the beef to a plate, reduce the heat to medium and add onions to the pot. Stir the onions in the pan to lift all the brown bits off the bottom of the pan and sauté until the onions begin to turn translucent. Add the meat back to the pot, placing the carrots and potatoes around it. Add ½ cup water, cover and put in the oven to bake.

Cook for 2 hours, check, stir and cook for another 1.5 hours. After 3.5 hours, remove the lid and bake for 1 more hour. For each additional ½ pound of meat over 4 pounds, increase the length of cooking time by a half an hour.

To serve: Remove ingredients to a deep casserole or serving bowl and cover loosely with foil. Leave liquid in Dutch oven, spooning off the fat, if desired. In a separate small bowl containing flour, remove ½ cup of the broth from the pot and stir into flour to make a thick, smooth paste. Pour this back into the pot and whisk to thicken remaining liquid into gravy. Pour over the serving bowl and serve.

Hogs

Along with chicken, hogs were easy to raise on the ranch for food. Eldora won't get into trouble for saying this now, so she told me she remembers playing in the cellar around large ceramic food storage crocks of salted pork and jars of cooked pork meat, usually bacon or chops, sealed in pork fat in jars. These jars of meat would keep as well as pickled vegetables, which is to say safely throughout the seasons. Next to the meat itself, the most valuable item from the hog was the lard rendered from it. This was possibly one of the least favorite times of year in the house, as processing lard in the kitchen produced a terrible, heavy odor until the fat was fully rendered. For a few days of temporary uninviting odors, the benefits of making lard from a hog were felt all year long; every time cakes, cookies or doughnuts were made, chicken was fried or food needed to be preserved, shelf-stable lard was the go-to fat. In the 1950s, vegetable shortening took hold, thanks to successful marketing campaigns claiming that it was healthier than lard. The campaigns worked, and lard was unseated as the most essential ingredient in the pantry. By the 1960s, lard had fallen out of favor and has only made a slight comeback today.

Butchering a hog would provide one family with two or three gallons of lard and at least a few hundred pounds of meat. Sausage was made, pattied, fried and packed in lard. Larger cuts would be stored for a short time unprocessed in cold-storage like cellars, but before mechanical refrigeration, they would typically be salted and packed in crocks. Pork meat holds up very well to salt as a preserver, so it was also brined in a salt solution and stored to be rinsed and used later. If families had access to a smokehouse, other cuts would be smoked. Small smokehouses could be made out of barrels but might be as large as a freestanding structure on the ranch. On the ranch, hogs are hardy, useful backstops for food waste. They will generally eat anything, reducing the need to buy feed for them on the farm. Nothing went to waste, even the waste itself.

Local Foods

For every person who recalls hunting and eating game such as deer and fowl, there's another who never made use of them as food items. Recipes for game are much more rare than recipes for domestically raised animals. When found, the recipes tend to be lumped in together and generically named, such as a "wild bird roast"—the bird being interchangeable. Hunters represent a small number of people who eat, and not all hunters hunt for food. The game recipes that appear in cookbooks or family histories have always been fringe pantry items in the shadows of more popular and available ingredients like pork, chicken, beef and grains.

Acts such as the Timber Culture Act had benefits beyond windbreaks and shade for humans. Since the Sand Hills became inhabited by settlers, deer have become more and more abundant in the Sand Hills region as trees planted by previous generations became established. Trees create habitats for wildlife to live and breed. Recipes for venison didn't tend to appear in cookbooks until specialty sections appeared for "game." Venison, while lean and having a slightly gamey flavor, is abundant (and one could argue overly so) in the Sand Hills, and it is likely the most popular game meat on tables today.

Prairie chicken were in such abundance when the first white settlers arrived that original Sand Hills settlers describe the hills as swarming with them, skies black with birds. The Sand Hills' high water table provides a tremendous natural refuge for migratory birds; tall grasses and ample fresh water create an environment for almost any land or water fowl. From this seemingly endless supply, people saw opportunity; the prairie chicken was culled along with pheasant, grouse and duck and shipped via rail into larger cities like Omaha, where the demand was high for fresh, wild birds. On occasion, the birds were not even shipped dressed but simply shipped whole, with entrails and feathers intact, shipped only on ice. In the *Mullen Roundup* in the early 1900s, businessman Elmer Lowe from Hyannis shipped fifty thousand birds on ice in a peak year.

By 1905, a game law limiting hunters to ten birds per day had taken effect to help stabilize the population. Today, fifty thousand prairie chickens do not exist on the planet. Some estimates suggest that there are only a few thousand left, a low enough number to be a candidate to be added to the U.S. Fish and Wildlife Threatened Species list. Just a few respites for the species exist in the Sand Hills, the National Wildlife Refuge in Cherry County and on the Switzer Ranch, a private working cattle ranch in Garfield County that has set aside land to preserve breeding grounds. During the dramatic (and lively) mating ritual displays, they regularly see two to three hundred chickens during this time.

Pheasant, on the other hand, enjoyed an upward population trajectory in the Sand Hills. Originally an Asian ground bird species, they came to the North American continent from Asia in 1733, to New York specifically. A

Garfield County Roundup reported that the first introduction of pheasant into the area was extremely successful. Originally introduced to the Sand Hills in about 1909, by 1919 they were considered "abundant." In 1928, thirty-five thousand pheasants were taken in one ten-day hunting season. Pheasant recipes began appearing in cookbooks shortly after their introduction but were generally very simple—stewed, roasted, fried and, on occasion, smoked. The birds are still prolific in the Sand Hills, as it is similar to the birds' native environments of tall grasses and rolling hills.

Duck and goose hunting has always been popular in the Sand Hills, since dozens of species of each migrate through the region every year. Of all the game, duck generally has its own recipes, since it is a more delicate bird with little gamey flavor. Geese are currently prolific in the Sand Hills and are relatively easy to hunt but tend to have an even gamier flavor than ducks and so end up lumped into "game" recipes.

Recipes for fowl tend to have them dressed, cleaned and roasted. Small birds like dove, quail, pigeon and Cornish hen appear together in many cases with one roasting time and temperature. Larger birds like goose, pheasant and duck have longer roast times, owing to their size, and also appear clustered together roasted in skillets or baking dishes.

The chokecherry holds a special place in Sand Hills pantries. It's a native plant that has existed for centuries on the land. Native migratory peoples and permanent settlers alike found and harvested the small, sour red berries for food. Raw, they are very tart and sometimes bitter, but they are full of fiber and antioxidants. The chokecherry bush or tree can reach fifteen feet in diameter and grows in abundance on slopes of hills with nearby water sources. Like other wild edibles such as wild plum, sand cherries and mulberries, it proliferates in the Sand Hills' sandy, dry soil. By this point, most ranchers know where they have thickets of berries, if they have them, and will harvest the fruits typically to be made into jellies or jams and preserved.

Every year, Sargent holds a popular Chokecherry Jamboree to celebrate the humble fruit. The festival invites participants to sell chokecherry plants, as well as foods such as jams, pies, jellies, pastries and sauces. It's a community event filled with games and attracts hundreds of visitors each year. The chokecherry was considered (and perhaps still is) a badge of a true salt-of-the-earth homesteader, representing foraging on the land for food. The bounty from chokecherry harvests arrives in early summer at farmers' markets, grocery stores and in trades of jars of preserves between friends and neighbors.

....

CHOKECHERRY JELLY (COURTESY STEPHANIE BIXBY GRAHAM)
Makes 12 pints

INGREDIENTS
4 cups chokecherry juice (about a bucket of whole berries to make)
1 box Sure-Jell pectin
5½ cups sugar

METHOD
Wash berries and put in water to cover. Bring to boil and simmer until berries begin to burst, about 20 minutes. Strain through cheesecloth. Mix Sure-Jell with juice in a large saucepan. Bring to a hard boil, stirring occasionally. Add sugar and bring to boil again for 1 minute, stirring constantly. Remove from heat, skim foam and pour into scalded jelly jars. Cap and let cool.

In 1930, there were 129,458 Nebraska farms listed in the USDA Census of Agriculture.

THE CREAM CHECK AND EGG MONEY

In cattle country, there is no disputing that cattle raised for beef is king. But another cow was equally as important to establishing the ranch way of life: dairy cows. They were relatively easy to keep, and as long as they were milked every day, they produced plenty of fresh cream. One cow could reliably produce about five gallons of milk per day. Anything cream is used for today, it was used then, with one exception: money. Cream was a commodity as good as currency almost until 1970. If men's income and the income for the ranch was made from cattle, women had an income as well: selling cream to milk exchanges. This, along with "egg money," might be considered women's first earned income. So often was it turned around and used to buy groceries that the "cream check," the check given as payment for cream sold to an exchange, became synonymous with "grocery money."

Isla's farm had a few dairy cows on it, and as a child, her least favorite job was cleaning the milk separator, a device separating heavier cream from lighter skim milk. She'd trade other chores to get out of it, blissfully unaware that cream separating was an income-producing chore on the farm. Her mother, however, was keenly aware of its importance as a pantry staple used to feed five children, her husband and any help on the farm. Isla cleaned the cream separator after her mother milked the cows, and they would take the cream in five-gallon containers, or "cream cans," into the cream exchange, often located in the backs of grocery markets. Isla's family usually took their cream to the Strong Market in Taylor to sell, but in neighboring Burwell, fifteen miles away, there were two cream exchanges. One was in the back of

Quartered   CONTENTS ONE POUND NET

Sweet Clover
Special
Butter

BURWELL BUTTER FACTORY, INC.,   BURWELL, NEBRASKA

The Burwell Butter Factory produced butter until its closing in 1974.

Udell Feeds, where Keith Udell opened a cream exchange in the back of his family's feed store.

The most important part of the process was administering a Babcock Test, determining the fat content in the cream to be sold. If the results fell within an acceptable range, the milk was purchased on the spot, and Udell Feeds would issue a check for the amount that corresponded to the amount of fat present in the cream. It was then put in a holding tank, and every Sunday, it was driven to a creamery in Grand Island, Nebraska, eighty-five miles away. In the 1930s, that was a two-hour journey each way. By 1950, the same trip took about an hour and a half each way.

Built into this errand of exchanging cream for the cream check was an exciting social time. Many ranch families brought their cream in on Saturday. "We'd take our cream into the exchange, get our cream can back and take our check over to the grocery store and buy groceries," Isla recalls. "Then we'd leave the groceries in the empty cream can at the market and go walk around the square for a night out." She adds, "We could leave stuff out and come back for it when we were ready. It was like that back then." Saturday nights were festive nights capturing both utility in completing chores and providing amusement and a chance to socialize. It was the one night when people who lived on remote ranches could still do errands and also enjoy a town dance, movie, a walk around the square or a drink at the bar. After the evening was over, everyone grabbed their milk can and rode by buggy home

17362

BURWELL BUTTER FACTORY, INC.
BURWELL, NEBRASKA

Date_____196_____

Lbs. of Cream_____ Test_____

Lbs. of Fat_____ Price_____

Amount_____

Corrections_____

Total_____

Mom & Dad Boggs

A receipt for selling cream dated August 1968. Most Sandhillers I spoke with remember the late 1960s being the last point in time they made such exchanges, usually because ranches got rid of their dairy cows or because exchanges closed or quit taking small batches of cream. *Irene Nelson Walker Collection.*

(or drove in later years). For many ranch wives and families, this was the only trip one would make to town in a week's (or longer) time.

Some ranches were so far from town that it wasn't practical to travel to make the exchange. These ranchers employed the one person whose job it was to make deliveries: the postal carrier. "This must have been what it cost to post it," Delores said, as we looked through her Great Uncle Gus's handwritten columns in his ledgers. He kept detailed records of his sales to the cream exchange in Valentine. We scrolled through pages of notes detailing the fat contents, amounts and prices earned from selling, from three dollars to six

Gus Wendler kept meticulous records of every aspect of the ranch. This cream log notes the date, Babcock Test number, fat percentage, cost to mail and amount received for the cream. *Ledger courtesy of Dean and Delores Colburn.*

dollars per shipment. The cost of sending a five-gallon can of cream forty miles into town in the 1930s was thirty-five cents. Max and Gus Wendler spent years faithfully delivering their liquid parcels to town. Three dollars in 1930, when adjusted for inflation, amounts to about forty dollars today, enough to provide a small but steady source of income on ranches.

At one time, it seemed that everyone was in the raw cream trade. As long as the milk cows were healthy, it was a reliable source of income for farmers and ranchers. Even the Union Pacific Railway Company was in the game. Its Land Department published a leaflet in the late 1880s explaining existing methods of dairying and how to make the most profit from them. If it seems odd that the railroad would publish a document about dairying, it is useful to remember the railroads had a tremendous stake in goods to be shipped in and out of their stations; they depended on trade of valuable items needed in various points across the country.

"Back then, we put cream on our cereal in the morning, not the stuff they have now," Eldora remembers. She doesn't prefer the texture and flavor of milk today. Isla's son, Tom, also remembers raw milk fondly. "My father would sit down at the farm table and pour himself a bowl of cornflakes from the box. He'd spoon on a heaping spoonful of cream right off the top of the can—the good stuff—and sprinkle a little sugar on it…It was like putting frosting on top of cereal."

As early as the 1940s, this milk began to be regularly pasteurized for consumption, a process by which it is heated to a certain temperature for a short duration of time to kill "harmful" bacteria. Many are relieved that milk is now pasteurized, but you'll still find a good number who lament the deterioration of milk as a product. "Raw was what we grew up on," says Tammy Rowse, "and we're just fine." Part Sand Hills resilience, part discounting a seemingly superfluous step in an otherwise simple process, it's a healthy skepticism of large dairies separating and pasteurizing a product and selling it back to ranchers. Well into the 1970s, dairy cows were still being milked on farms, and while some home pasteurizing machines were available, most still milked the way they always had, with no need for pasteurization. Today, finding raw milk in the Sand Hills is more like setting out on a treasure hunt than it is checking off a grocery list item. Not many people keep dairy cows anymore since they must be milked twice a day, and there is no longer anywhere to sell the milk. The consolidation of the dairy industry onto factory farms all but eliminated the small-batch sale.

Raw milk's disappearance changed the shape of baked goods in the kitchen, literally as well as figuratively. Full cream adds an unmistakable richness to baked goods, but it makes them heavier and denser, which leaveners can only partially counteract. For pastry, this isn't always ideal. In the 1930s, recipes that called for "cream" meant it; it was a measure of "top milk," the cream that naturally separated to the top after sitting for a few hours. With the process of pasteurization also came the choice of lighter fat percentages. Today, the cream (containing most of the fat) is separated out and a certain percentage of fat solids added back, creating our commonly known fat percentages of 1 percent, 2 percent and whole. Half-and-half is half milk, half cream, with a fat percentage of upward of 10 percent. The whole cream that families drank for decades on the farm could have had fat percentages of 35 percent and up. If the adage "fat is flavor" is true, it certainly helps explain why many Sand Hills residents remember things tasting better in the past. Palates adjusted to the change that lighter milks made in pastry, and today, we tend to expect lighter, fluffier pastry that lower-fat milks provide.

Waste is actually a four-letter word in the Sand Hills. From recipes using up soured milk to those created by using the discard of yeast starter, nothing—and I mean *nothing*—goes to waste on a Sand Hills ranch. Recipes for leftover mashed potatoes turned into the next morning's fried potato patties. Hogs were fed with the skim milk leftover from the cream separator. Stews stretched anything—potatoes, egg noodles or meat left on bones. All of these are foods that were eaten and recipes made in the Sand Hills.

On one of my many visits with Eldora, she mentioned using cream before it went sour. I asked, "What happened if it did?" She said, "Well, you'd cook with it before it spoiled!" It was a moment in the interview where I didn't want to appear as if I didn't know what she was talking about—the difference between "soured" and "spoiled"—so I made a note of it to research later. Soured milk pops up in old recipe books more often than newer ones, so I suspected it had something to do with raw milk.

I called my raw milk connection, donated some more money to his cows, set a bowl of raw milk next to my stove and left it there overnight. By the end of the next evening, it had thickened in texture and smelled sour. A few days after that, it smelled "off." Soured milk happens in a short window of fermentation in the life of raw milk before it goes bad. I grew up on pasteurized milk my entire life, which doesn't acidify (sour) first. Pasteurizing milk kills the bacteria—good and bad—that allow for the fermentation process that causes souring, so it goes straight to spoilage when left out. Once I started working with soured cream—the "real," raw stuff—I didn't want to live without it once I left my Sand Hills milk connection, so I use the following ratio in pasteurized milk to re-create the flavor of it.

•••

SOURED CREAM
Makes 1 cup

INGREDIENTS
1 cup organic heavy cream, not ultra-pasteurized
1 tablespoon lemon juice

METHOD
In a large glass or ceramic bowl, whisk together the cream and lemon juice. Place in the refrigerator, covered, for 30 minutes, during which time the cream will thicken.

To use: Use soured milk one-for-one in any recipe that calls for milk or cream. I use it liberally in the recipes in this book, from soured whipped cream topping short cakes to a marinade for the fried chicken. To replicate soured milk, I prefer to sour with lemon juice, although the same measure of white vinegar will do.

To whip: Cream with a hand mixer on medium-high speed until soft peaks form, about 5–6 minutes. Cover and place back in the refrigerator until use.

EGGS

Along with cream for the exchange, Tom has vivid memories of taking eggs to the grocery store in the 1960s with his mother, Isla. They drove to the town square in Taylor, and the owner of the store would pay him a dime, sometimes a quarter, to repackage the day's haul of eggs into larger commercial crates used to transport the eggs. It was big money for a child at the time. Eggs were (and to some extent still can provide) extra pocket change on the farm. Women in kitchens would use as many eggs as they needed and sell any surplus to the grocery store in town for a little extra "egg money." Many would raise chickens specifically for the egg money to help offset the cost of groceries. Along with the industrialization of milk, eggs went along with it when it became cheaper and easier to buy factory-grown versions at the store than to keep the chickens to produce them. On occasion, you'll still see signs for "farm fresh eggs" in feed stores, hardware stores and the markets in the Sand Hills.

"Those eggs are standing up well," Eldora says, looking through pictures of farm eggs frying in a pan I took at a breakfast my aunt and uncle in Valentine made for me on a visit. Not much has changed in how a good egg is judged: a thick, strong shell containing a dark-orange yolk that stands very firm when cracked open has always been the mark of a good farm egg. In the past decade, laying hens have had a resurgence in popularity, making appearances again on ranches and farms and even turning up in urban backyards. They don't take much work to keep, but they do need consistent care to be productive. Eggs are an easy source of protein and are an ingredient that is as easily prepared alone or used to stretch other dishes.

EGG NOODLES

Egg noodles are simple to make in any size batch, and this makes them an ideal go-to recipe to stretch a meal. As much counter space as you're willing to devote to them is how many egg noodles you can make by simply doubling or tripling the ingredients. They are cheap, easy, use only four ingredients and can be dried and stored for future meals. Versions of egg noodle recipes pop up in many cookbooks of all types, and almost every German and Polish immigrant cookbook I came across has a version. Regardless of ancestry, their ability to stretch a recipe to feed a large family with few ingredients makes it another ranch kitchen essential. Egg noodles can be eaten on their own as butter noodles or added to soups, stews and roasts to give those dishes more heft. It's hard to mess with perfection. After testing a number of recipes, they all pretty much come down to a ratio.

. . . . .

Makes two batches, or about 1 pound of noodles

INGREDIENTS
1½ to 2 cups flour, sifted
1 teaspoon salt
2 large farm-fresh eggs, room temperature
¼ cup heavy cream

METHOD
Place flour in a mound on a cutting board. Sprinkle salt across the top. Make a well large enough for the eggs. Add eggs to the well and break them up slightly with a fork. Add ¼ cup cream and mix with your hands and spatula or bowl scraper until the dough comes together. Add enough flour for the dough to become extremely firm and no longer sticky. Knead for 2 minutes or until the dough has a smooth texture.

Divide dough in half and knead each half back into a ball. Wrap each ball tightly in plastic wrap and let rest in the refrigerator for 30 minutes. Remove from refrigerator and, working one half at a time, knead the ball for 30 seconds and roll out to ⅛ inch thick on the cutting board, making sure to keep it floured. With a knife or a pizza cutter, cut into ¼-inch strips about 3 inches long, toss them to separate and let rest for 30 minutes before using. The noodles can be dried and stored in the refrigerator for up to two weeks, but they are best used immediately by boiling or adding to soup or stew.

BUTTER

"I remember one customer riding in a buggy into town with a can of cream," Keith Udell recalls. "The roads were so bad that when he arrived at the store, it had already been churned into butter." When it doesn't happen by accident, churning between two and three gallons of whole milk steadily for twenty minutes, followed by ten minutes of "finishing" work with a paddle on a cutting board, will make about one pound of butter. A specialized piece of equipment on the ranch called a butter churn made easy if time-consuming work of it. It is now a staple fat in the kitchen, but it had a slow start into pantries. Printed recipes don't begin using it until around the 1940s, perhaps coincidentally after most homes were electrified. Butter would keep for a week or two chilled, while a crock of rendered lard, if stored properly, will keep for months. Many people prefer the flavor of butter, but lard has a higher smoke point, meaning frying with it was possible. And unlike lard, butter could not be used as a preservative for other foods. Lard was practical in kitchens, but butter had one simple advantage over lard: flavor. It was pastry's best friend, lending a sweet, creamy richness to any dish.

Right behind the industrialization of milk after World War II came the mass industrialization of butter, making it more readily available in grocery stores. Today, the art of hand-churning has all but disappeared; it is cost- and time-prohibitive to make your own. The price of three gallons of milk to make a pound of butter far exceeds the cost of one pound of store-bought butter on the shelf. Despite the fact that small amounts of butter can be made in home stand mixers, for the time involved, making butter is a losing venture. Outside of reminiscing or seeing if the old churn in storage still works, very few people make it for personal use today.

"You know what they don't have anymore around here?" says Marvin "Murph" Murphy, born and raised in Rock and Garfield Counties. "Buttermilk-fed hogs. You'll never find anything like it again." His family raised them on their land in Rock County. In the 1950s, Murph remembers driving into Burwell with his father and loading up cream cans and fifty-gallon drums with buttermilk drawn from a hose off the back of the Burwell Butter Factory. The factory was the only butter manufacturing facility for a hundred miles. It opened in 1916 and bought cream from farmers and ranchers to make butter with until the day it closed its doors in 1974. Buttermilk is a byproduct of making butter, and the factory sold it for pennies on the gallon to anyone who wanted it since it was considered factory waste.

As long as dairy cows were on the farm, pigs regularly enjoyed a steady diet of leftover cream or skim milk, making the description "milk-fed hog" a repetitive statement. Skim milk that was separated from the cream in separators never made it into the house; it was considered waste and fed to the hogs. Today, milk-fed hogs, supplemented with buttermilk or otherwise, have gone the way of the dairy cow.

In 1945, there were 111,756 Nebraska farms listed in the USDA Census of Agriculture.

ADVANCE AND DECLINE

The Great Depression

The very things that make life out in the Sand Hills difficult are the same things that protect it from hardship. The remote, self-sufficient, agriculturally based way of life in the 1930s operated much more as a barter economy than in urban areas. Less physical money was changing hands, and when it did, the investments were durable and could be seen in cattle or landholdings. The stock market, centralized in New York, was more focused on stocks than on futures or commodities trading, so when the bottom fell out of the paper economy, it was slower to affect the more resilient economy of the Sand Hills. This is not to say that the Sand Hills did not endure tremendous hardships caused by the Great Depression. The layer of insulation that the Sand Hills way of life provided was a very thin one, and cattle prices still dropped by 66 percent. The government was paying ranchers to destroy herds to keep them from flooding the market. The price of cattle went through the floor. In 1920, a head of cattle would sell for about fifty dollars. In 1932, the price dropped to nineteen dollars. With prices that low, it was difficult to generate income to keep ranching operations afloat.

The railroads, a symbol of connection to the rest of the country, brought signs of how bad the conditions were outside the Sand Hills. "As children, we didn't know we were in the Depression because everyone else was in the same way," Eldora says. "But we were never hungry because we always had our own chickens and could fish and always had a pig for meat." If the Depression didn't fully grip the Sand Hills, hints of it were seen on the outskirts. At twelve years old, Eldora developed a goiter, and the closest doctor to remedy it was outside the Sand Hills in Grand Island, more than eighty miles away. The drive there crossed a set of railroad tracks in heavy use transporting goods back and forth across the country. "Somehow, some of the boxcars were overturned on the tracks, and we got to within a couple hundred feet of the track before we had to stop. There were so many men wandering in the fields, we began counting them. We counted ninety bums got out of the train." Eldora says that the train crews at that time only amounted three or four people: "The engineer, a conductor, and someone to shovel coal." It was her first indication that something was wrong, seeing so many men hitching rides on the rails to seek work in other towns. "Cars carrying potatoes and apples were upset, and I watched them [the men] stuff their pockets full of them."

Eldora's family's ranch was upriver from the end of a rail line. The Depression era was the only time Eldora remembers seeing men from outside the Sand Hills wandering onto their ranch and asking for food and a place to stay. Men would ride the rails to the end of the line and walk up the river, looking for ranches that had any work. Her father obliged, letting travelers work for room and board "until they got set up again and would walk back to the end of the line and be on their way." It was a common enough event at the time that her father kept an extra bed in the basement and on the screened-in porch during summers.

For all of the years that settlers may have cursed the sandy soil, its natural crop, hay, grew every year, whether desired or not. That fact and irrigation for fields have been the Sand Hills' continual insulator from outside market forces. Other parts of the Great Plains did not fare as well. In the Great Plains and in the Sand Hills, the "Dirty Thirties," coined as a description due to the incessant dust blowing from drought and overplowing in the region, were filled with insect plagues; hot, dry winds; and eroding confidences. By all accounts, no one had any money, so neighbors helped one another in times of emergency and struggle.

In the 1930s, what money and crops that were available elsewhere dried up and blew away. Eldora met her husband in the ruins of it. "It was his first year out of high school [in Kansas], and he put a crop in on a neighbor's land," she remembers. "The corn got halfway to his knees and then died." The grasses in the Sand Hills, on the other hand, are extremely drought tolerant, so *something* will grow every year. As long as cattle feed on the grasses, there will be something to take to market. "He heard there was hay up north on the low ground near the streams, and it was irrigated out of the valleys." Norman "Red" Muirhead made the trip north to Nebraska in 1935, to Cascade, where Eldora's family's ranch was. They met in 1938 and married in 1940.

The sandy hills and the prairie grasses also insulated the region from the extreme effects of drought and what would come to be known as the "Dust Bowl." Lands as close as three hundred miles away were aggressively overplowed and planted during the rapid expansion west. With drought destroying crops, there was nothing to hold down the topsoil that had been tilled. It was blowing away in a dangerous and epic fashion in the hot winds, destroying previously arable farmland. The Dust Bowl drove people off the land not only from the financial devastation but also from the physical peril of breathing in dust, day after day. The dust got into the flour, the pantries— just about every crevice of daily life. Sand Hills settlers learned very early that the land could not be plowed, so the mighty grasslands remained intact.

Many areas of the country were suffering the darkness of the Depression, but meanwhile, the Sand Hills were lighting up, literally, with the benefit of electricity.

ELECTRICITY

One sign that your recipe research is exhaustive is finding a recipe for light. An old, spiral-bound circa 1963 Czech heritage cookbook contained a recipe for a homemade lamp, and of course, I had to test it. If any recipe highlights the spirit of resourcefulness and the utility of plains settlers, it's this one. And the recipe works:

> *Did you know that—Pioneer women used buttons to create makeshift lamps. A piece of cloth was tied around a button and cut about an inch above. The cloth was immersed in fat and set in a saucer of oil. It would burn brightly.* –Kucharka Ceska

The Sand Hills, like many of the country's remote areas, were wired for electricity relatively late, keeping candlepower in use much longer than in urban areas. Nearby cities like Omaha and Denver began to electrify as early as the 1880s, but the farther out from dense urban areas, the longer it took to convince local governments of the need to invest in power lines.

This was the most unusual recipe test! Made from a piece of cloth, a metal button and two tablespoons of olive oil set in a ceramic ramekin, this candle burned for about three hours. I'd recommend setting it on a trivet when lit.

In 1930, almost 90 percent of all urban Americans had electricity in their homes. In rural areas, only 10 percent did. By now, most farmhouses also had indoor plumbing, a vast improvement from the outhouse, but it took an act of government to electrify rural areas. In 1935, the Rural Electrification Act passed, allowing public utility companies to form and provide low-cost services to smaller customer bases in hard-to-reach areas.

Irene Nelson Walker was born in a farmhouse deep in the Sand Hills of Garfield County. She attended a country school (as opposed to coming into

Burwell's town school) in Garfield County in the Sunnyside District, and growing up, she lived the first years of her life in a sod house on the property that her parents owned. They moved a wooden house onto the property in about 1950 that, to this day, does not have electricity. It sits uninhabited, still "poking its head out from the trees." Irene never cared that she didn't have electricity in the country, even though she knew the kids who lived in town did. Kids who came out from the city would wander up a hill out back of the wooden house and roll or slide down it. It was plenty of distraction to keep them happy. By the end of the day, they were full of sand, exhausted and hungry.

The fact that electricity was becoming a public service was no concern to a few resilient Sand Hills ranchers. Ranches began acquiring and installing self-contained "light plants" powered by wind generators or fossil fuel sources for as many as twenty years before the act passed. Eldora remembers her family's first electricity in the 1930s, before public wired infrastructure was built, in the form of a "Delco light plant," a propane-powered system that charged a series of batteries. It was a low-voltage system that powered a few light bulbs and appliances like electric irons and fans made specifically for the unit. The light plants didn't affect kitchens much more than adding a light bulb to the room. Delco had a model designed specifically for farms that included enough wiring to place light bulbs in outbuildings, where light after dark was helpful when chores ran late.

Public power may have entered the home, but it didn't mean the lights stayed on. Dean and Delores installed a wind charger before public lines came onto their ranch and have always been prepared with two backup generators (one for the house and another for outbuildings) whenever they lose public power. Electricity brought convenience into kitchens and the rest of the world into homes. Radios, and later televisions, became attainable electronics. If each ranch is a "floating island," the lines began to change that by tethering residents together in the Sand Hills.

When ranches became wired, it brought the biggest improvement rural kitchens have seen to date: the refrigerated appliance. It changed the entire process of food preparation in the kitchen. Food would stay reliably cold until the power went out. If cream lasted forty-eight hours in a cellar or cistern in the 1920s, a family was lucky. With the refrigerator, it was possible to extend fresh cream's life to three or four days, an impossibility before this invention. Refrigerators were usually placed on the main floors, in kitchens, dining rooms or lean-tos outside the kitchen, so ranch women no longer had to climb up and down narrow stairways into dirt cellars for food. In the same room or just nearby, one could now store, retrieve and cook with ingredients, simplifying tasks and reducing worry about food spoilage.

Even with refrigeration, alternative food preservation methods such as canning are still very popular in the Sand Hills. A number of factors might explain it: The culture galvanized around self-sufficiency, so having a full pantry is a result of that. Electricity came late to the Sand Hills, so it would also make sense that food preservation skills are later to disappear. Gardening skills are still second nature, and the bounty from tending them is essentially free. The investment in preservation is time and money for reusable jars, far less than buying the same amount of jarred foods at the store. Taste is subjective, but almost everyone I spoke with believes that home-canned fruits or vegetables taste better than store bought, and there's a fierce loyalty to this perception of flavor, especially in an agricultural area, where gardens are historically significant. Having eaten the bounty of Sand Hills gardens, it's hard to argue with that sentiment. The flavors of three-hour-old potatoes and spinach cut the same morning are fuller and more vibrant.

Once kitchens were fully electrified, ranch wives had a flood of handheld and countertop appliances marketed to them like toasters, hand mixers and electric coffeepots. With the advent of hand mixers alone, whipped cream and meringues became more popular in cookbooks. Blenders pureed soups. What had previously been manual jobs were done in less than half the time with electricity. One of Isla's favorite improvements from when electricity entered the kitchen was the toaster. The appliance made a simple act of freshening a piece of bread much easier without having to start a large oven to accomplish it. Ranch kitchens were indeed moving forward, but the area was nevertheless in steady but silent decline.

1935

When Isla graduated high school in 1935, she was unable to find a teaching job in the area, so she took a "fifth year" of high school, increasing her skills in typing and English to improve her chances for a good position the following year. The next year, she successfully retained a teaching position in Loup County. Neither Isla nor Eldora could know that the year was a very important one for the Sand Hills and the state of Nebraska—it was the year the Sand Hills would be the most densely populated in its history. In 1935, Nebraska saw the highest population of rural farms and

An abandoned homestead in Garfield County.

residents it would ever see. The USDA Census of Agriculture reported 133,616 farms in the state.

Farm and ranch consolidation has always been a part of the Great Plains and the Sand Hills. It started right after the first homestead claims were made. Across the country, just 40 percent of the claims successfully proved up. In the early days, failure to raise and sell cattle at market caused people to move on for more fertile or workable ground. Those who were able to put small crops on land that was dense enough to till had some income at harvest time, but they were subject to the annual agricultural challenges of drought, pests and disease. Mechanical appliances that saved time and effort in the kitchens were welcome devices, but there was a downside to saving labor. Mechanization happened in all aspects of ranch life, bringing more efficient tractors to mow grass and more effective bailing machines. Each of those improvements in technology cut a manual laborer out of the process. In the 1930s, a haying crew contained six men. By 1960, they needed only three to complete the same amount of work—or more.

"Out here, there used to be a house on every section," Isla's son, Tom, remembers about the Sand Hills. If they were in the same room, Delores could have finished his sentence. "Now it's harder to get help for branding

The remnants of the general store in Brownlee, Cherry County.

anymore." Brandings used to bring one hundred people to feed and required at least five ranch wives working together to pull it off. Today, Delores will feed thirty-five people—no small amount, but much smaller than the same event on the same land fifty years before.

WORLD WAR II

Eldora's biggest concern during the war was not food rationing. That problem was mostly contained in the cities. Her biggest challenge with the ration coupons was the paltry two pairs of shoe stamps she received each year for her children. It remained in the back of her mind until one day, she found her son walking in the pasture without shoes. "He saw a rabbit in the grass and remembered at Easter, the Easter Bunny hid eggs in his shoes. So, he thought if he took his shoes off and left them, the rabbit would come back and put eggs in his shoes." He left his shoes in the sea of grass and wandered through the pasture, barefoot. It was a moment of panic for Eldora until they found the shoes, since for growing farm children, two pairs were barely enough to cover growing feet.

Sand Hills kitchens were almost untouched by wartime. The popular government Victory Garden campaign targeted areas that didn't have gardens or didn't already grow their own food to start planting gardens. The areas that needed food in their backyards were dense urban areas that sacrificed garden space for living space. The movement included a push for more community gardens and for people to devote patches of backyards, schoolyards and vacant lots to the production of food to reduce the domestic need for it, freeing up products for government export to aid the war effort. "We didn't need Victory Gardens on the ranches because we already had them. They were putting those in towns," Eldora remembers. In the Sand Hills, gardens much larger than the suggested size of Victory Gardens were already in place and had been sustaining families for decades. Ration and Victory Garden cookbooks that sprung up as a byproduct of the campaign didn't take up much real estate on bookshelves in the Sand Hills as a result.

Rations restricted people's ability to purchase or acquire items for their households. There was only one food generated that the War Office required citizens to turn in. Eldora and many other ranch wives faithfully turned in their cans of used bacon grease to War Offices in towns across the country. It contained glycerin that could be extracted to make dynamite. If anything, the biggest shortage to hit the Sand Hills was grown men. As eligible, adult males flocked to enlist in the armed forces and serve their country, they left behind gaping holes in the workloads of ranches.

By World War II, the drought that had gripped the 1930s had let up, and rains returned to the Great Plains. Tall grasses, hay fields and gardens flourished with the return of moisture. Life in the kitchen and gardens remained physically unchanged, if emotionally more difficult knowing that so many young men were subject to the perils of war. Some of these brave men never came home, creating new crises on the ranches.

By this time, the basic pantry had expanded to accommodate a full palate. Oranges from California were no longer luxuries, and tinned fish like tuna and sardines were readily available at the markets. Flour and cornmeal was no longer milled by hand, coffee was available in stores already roasted and even ground and spices from all over the world could be found on store shelves. The options seemed only as limited as the money needed to buy them.

If time could freeze here, this era might have felt like the most bountiful the Sand Hills would ever be. Men returned from war, and rains returned to the land. The country was celebrating a global victory along with technological and industrial leaps forward. For a few years, the razor-thin margin of prosperity came down on the side of farmers and ranchers. In fact, time did freeze here, just long enough to kill thousands of cattle and stop Sand Hills residents in their tracks.

BLIZZARD OF 1949

Major weather events crash like waves in the Sand Hills. This present-day February, Delores didn't leave the house, much less the ranch, in sixteen days, as it was so bitterly cold. Just a month later in March, I drove onto the Rowse Ranch in Garfield County through another brutally cold storm. I passed a dead, frozen cow in one of the pastures. I kicked the snow off my ill-equipped boots on the ranch house porch and walked inside to visit Irene, the family's elder. Irene was standing at the door to help me inside. Her daughter, Tammy, was moving around in a frenzy wearing jeans, full chaps, a wool hat and a thick Carhartt jacket. Behind them lay a newborn calf in front of the fireplace in the living room.

The ranch's "hot boxes," protective rooms set up on the ranch for new mom and calf pairs, were full, and they were trying to get enough heat in the barn to start moving the new calves over into it. The ranch was caught between a very large calving season of 1,200 heifers and a bitterly cold snowstorm that killed livestock across the state. The storm was typical of a January storm, but this is March. It's prime calving season for a reason—it is supposed to be the end of winter. The entire family was out working cows, coming inside every half hour or so to warm up. If the color of Tammy's cheeks and nose were any indication, no amount of layers and adrenaline takes the sting out of twenty below. The best they could do for the animals was to bring newborns into the living room and put them on the floor in front of the fireplace to warm up. Many more came, but the storm killed almost fifty more. It was a difficult time on the ranch, but in everyone's memory, nothing is a comparison to the Sand Hills' most devastating storm: the winter blizzard of 1949.

It was the largest blizzard in recorded history to hit the Sand Hills. The blizzard threatened more than 1 million head of cattle across the region, covering the Sand Hills with a thick blanket of snow, creating snow drifts fifteen feet deep, trapping people on ranches and separating cattle from food and water sources. Eldora's sister, brother-in-law and their newborn baby were on their way to Valentine when the storm hit. "It was like a curtain came down over us, it hit [the region] so hard." They stopped at a ranch house along the way to seek shelter. They were snowed in at someone else's home for two weeks. "They used dishtowels as diapers for their little boy." Eldora remembers the stories of thousands of cattle lost to the blizzard, although they were lucky on their ranch and lost only a few cows. Through an effort called "Operation Haylift," both private and government planes combined to fly over ranches and drop hay to feed millions of cattle across the state. Millions of those cattle were saved, but thousands were lost in a time when beef prices were high. While waiting out the snowmelt on the ranch, she recalls, "The only two things I really wanted were yeast and the mail." It was three weeks before she got either.

Not all meals are authentic re-creations of past family recipes, but that doesn't mean they're made with any less care or intention. The night I visited the Rowse Ranch, we sat down to a baking dish of lasagne, potato salad and rolls brought over by friends, providing a hot, large, no-fuss meal for a family at a critical time on their ranch. Their friends' presences also lightened the load a little bit. Tammy and her husband, Jerry, when they're not running a large cattle operation, host guests in six cabins on the land. They run a "working ranch" experience, where visitors come and spend a week or more actively participating in ranch duties. One-third of their guests are international visitors eager to experience an American western lifestyle, right down to what's on the plate. The ranch certainly provides that, and Tammy continues that experience through the food on the table. Regular meals for these guests are Rowse family recipes, handed down through the generations.

Found recipes almost always have clues within them that help pinpoint their origins. Many old family recipes are for large amounts of food. Before farm consolidation and the technological improvements of the 1940s and '50s played a major part in reshaping the landscape, Sand Hills recipes were noticeably larger in size. Recipes written in amounts that fed ten to twelve hungry, hardworking people were probably written before the war, when farms and ranches were bigger and less mechanized. In the 1960s and beyond, recipes that served more than eight started appearing as "large batch" in church and club cookbooks. Today, a standard-sized recipe serves from four to six. In the 1930s, that would have been considered a half batch or less. Enter Eldora's grandmother's recipe for molasses cookies.

CHERRY COUNTY "SCHOOL" COOKIES

Another recipe Eldora recalled from memory was a batch of molasses cookies. Grandmother Hoefs would make them on the ranch and hand them out as treats every time the children would visit, sometimes after they rode the three miles home from school on horseback. Eldora listed the ingredients from memory and then added, "and enough flour to roll them out." Since I didn't know how much flour was used, my first clue indicating that the batch was going to be large was the generous measure of molasses. I immediately halved the batch. Even with this reduction, it still took 8 cups of flour to make workable cookie dough, and by the time I was finished rolling, cutting and baking, I had more than twelve dozen cookies flooding my kitchen counters.

I gave them away to neighbors and co-workers for days, making ice cream sandwiches with some to use two cookies in one serving. Thankfully, I tested this right before the holidays, so for every party I attended, I took at least a dozen to give to each host. A few months later, I told Eldora about the recipe test. "You made that entire batch?" I replied, "I made half of the batch, and I was up to my eyeballs in cookies!" She laughed. "My grandmother would make a batch of those in a dishpan, and it would last for three weeks on the ranch!" I can coin a new phrase: a Sand Hills dozen. A dozen dozens. Everything out here is about that big.

• •

Makes: 12 dozen cookies

Ingredients

2 cups sugar

1 cup lard

1½ cups soured cream (see recipe on page 92)

1½ cups molasses

3½ teaspoons baking soda

1½ teaspoons ginger

½ teaspoon salt

8–8½ cups plus bench flour to roll

Method

Preheat oven to 350°F. In a very large mixing bowl, add all ingredients except flour and stir to combine. With 1 cup at a time, add flour until a pliable (but not sticky) dough forms. Divide dough into eighths and roll out to ¼ inch thickness. Cut with a 3-inch round cookie cutter (or any desired shape). Place onto cookie sheets lined with parchment paper and bake two sheets at a time for 14–15 minutes, rotating the pans once during baking. Store in airtight containers for a week or freeze for a month.

INDUSTRIALIZATION

Postwar modernization in the Sand Hills kitchen was in full effect. After drought and war, ranching reached a momentary stasis. By the 1950s, almost all of the Sand Hills were electrified, and indoor plumbing was a certainty in farmhouses. Financial markets began to show the results of bringing America's men home from war—productivity of the country (and innovation) was at an all-time high. Ready-mix products like cakes, brownie mixes and pancake mix landed on store shelves and replaced the handmade versions in kitchens. Other new food inventions like vegetable shortening hit shelves, and the frozen "TV dinner" became a reality.

Most home cooks didn't notice the decline in railroad service because the rise of the automobile, along with improved roads and trucking, expanded their food choices in markets and general stores. More shipping of goods by using highways meant more and better roads were built. Families began purchasing cars at a record pace, giving people the freedom to travel farther and more comfortably on their own. Televisions entered homes and provided yet another lifeline—a window out to the rest of the country that brought food advertising to homes, creating demand for more convenient products like the ones seen on television.

Outside the kitchens, however, the decline of the railroads had very real implications. An industry that was once the pioneer of transportation and shipping was being chipped away by trucking and individuals' newfound desires to travel freely. In many ways, in kitchens and on ranches, the hard work had been done. The land was tamed, the benefits were being seen and the lure of convenient foods and faster preparation presented new and easier ways to get a ranch meal on the table.

"Convenience" food purchases increased as the population declined in the area and brought garden square footage down with it. With fewer people needing food, or fewer people around on ranches to tend a garden, garden space shrank, especially as people moved into towns. A sign of this shift is evident in the many recipes contained within extension club and church cookbook collections in the 1960s. Many were reprints from the backs of brand-name ingredient packages like Cool Whip, Baker's Chocolate, Royal Baking Powder and popular flour and sugar manufacturers. Others were taken directly from *McCall's*, *Reader's Digest* and other popular magazines of the time. Items like Betty Crocker Brownies, heavenly hash using Dole brand pineapple and Mrs. Fields chocolate chip cookies proliferated. In any plains kitchen, the origin of the information itself was not as important as the quality of information—if the recipe worked and the family liked it, it became a favorite recipe to be used for generations. Whether it was truly grandma's or a recipe from *McCall's* magazine was of little practical concern.

Even with the influx of convenience into kitchens, making do was—and in many ways still is—a way of life. What may have been stews and soups in the 1930s and 1940s became casseroles and "bakes" in the 1950s and 1960s. Pages in cookbooks that previously called for simmering pots became devoted to recipes put in the oven. Potato gratins, goulashes, "macaroni main dish pie," meat loaf, "Mexican chili dish" and "pork chop casserole" included the convenience of canned ingredients poured into dishes and baked. The convenience of a one-dish meal is undeniable, and women flocked to these time-saving recipes in kitchens.

There was no less of a demand for quality ingredients, but the 1960s brought challenges in acquiring them. By 1969, there were half the farms there were in 1935 in Nebraska. The people who owned them moved into towns or out of the area. Ingredients harvested from home gardens were harder to come by, and going to the store became easier. Almost everyone had an automobile at this point, and gasoline was cheap, effectively closing the distances between ranches and stores. Isla Emerton also thinks that this era was the start of the downfall of a very important and prized crop in the Sand Hills: the tomato. "I just can't find them like they used to taste anymore." Her recollection is echoed across the Sand Hills. Eldora would agree. "People will never know what a real tomato is supposed to taste like." She adds, "Now, they're red and hard. They bred them so they could ship them and sit on a store shelf and not spoil." The decline in flavor of the tomato could be from soil quality, seed quality, decline in gardening skills or a combination of all three. Whatever the case, like the buttermilk-fed hog, a tomato you could pick out of the garden and eat like an apple also seems to have been left in history.

This windmill pumps water to irrigate the established home garden of Bob and Karen Hudecek outside Valentine, Nebraska.

For every boom, there's a bust. The land weathered the cycles of wet years and droughts, great blizzards and plagues, but the most difficult event for the Sand Hills landowners was the farm crisis of the 1970s and 1980s. The boom started in the 1970s, when crop prices soared. Banks allowed farmers to borrow money on future high crop prices. Optimistic farmers jumped on the wave of lending. In the 1980s, crop and land prices fell, leaving behind mountains of farm and ranch debt, as well as bankruptcies. The 1980s became the intersection of falling land prices, exploding debt and farm consolidation. In almost every analysis, it was the hardest challenge the family farm faced, and for many farms, it would be their last.

In 1950, there were 107,183 Nebraska farms listed in the USDA Census of Agriculture. From here forward, Nebraska would lose almost 10,000 farms every five years until 1969, when the census reported 72,257 farms. By 2007, there were 49,969 farms left in the state.

THE NEXT GENERATION

Global, economic and social events tend to lap up at the isolated edges of the Sand Hills, rippling slowly across the hills like gentle waves. In a relatively short time in this country's history, the Sand Hills filled with permanent settlers in search of free land and a new start from which to build better lives for themselves and their families. The hills were settled, towns built, the area reached peak population and began its decline as crop prices went down and land prices went up.

The Sand Hills never made the leap from rural to urban environment. The shifting sands wouldn't have supported it anyway. Still, every generation brings new pioneers. Although fewer in number, the area is steeped in generations of independent spirits and problem-solvers full of unflinching work ethics and self-sufficiency. In this remoteness comes its source of resilience and optimism.

"This is a joke to people, really," Delores's son, Keith, says as he looks out over the large pens containing ten sows, as well as one boar off in his own section. He rotates these pigpens twice a year and trucks in new, clean sand to replace the old. A large building divided up into pens containing ten litters of at least ten piglets each is behind us. The piglets are free to roam in and out, but they're all inside today, chittering at one another and competing for space to stay warm under the heat lamps. "No one raises hogs like this anymore. Most pigs live their entire lives in sheds. Their feet never touch the ground."

Every year, Keith raises 150 or so "sand hogs"—his own affectionate term, as he hasn't really thought about what else he'd call them. They started out as a supplement to ranch income, and it seems like he wasn't expecting to be so successful in the hog business. Half of the 150-some piglets staying warm in the shed are already sold to waiting customers, eager to eat all-natural, stress-, antibiotic- and hormone-free meat. The shed doesn't smell. "These little guys are toilet trained." They're essentially free-range animals; when it's cold like this, Keith lets them out into pigpens twice a day to change the hay in the pens inside to keep it clean. He moves clean sand into existing pens and rotates the herd on the ranch to keep the impact on the land low.

"Pigs are smart. Smarter than cows, I think," Irene tells me. She, along with many others who have lived a ranch life, had similar experiences as Keith raising hogs. Pigs are actually quite clean animals if left to their own devices. Even so, Keith is like clockwork with his daily schedule tending them. The piglets will do their business outside along the fences of the pigpens where they roam until they feel like wandering back in to the warmth that the glowing heat lamps hovering over each pen provide. The piglets know where to go when they want to go in; they always find their way back with their own siblings. The sows have numbers painted on their backs that correspond to the pens inside so other members of the Colburn family know which sow belongs to which litter, but Keith says it's really not necessary; a sow might wander into a different pen, but she'll immediately come out and enter the pen with her own litter for feeding. Keith helps the sows out by bottle-feeding any of the runts.

Dean, his father, says about industrialized hog farming, "If you go into one of those factory sheds, you'll come out smelling like ammonia for days. There's no way that can't get into the hog, living its entire life there." He chuckles when I ask about Keith's hogs. "They live a low-stress life," he says. "I know they are free range because once in a while we will look out the window and see Keith driving them to new ground." They can be herded simply by a few people walking behind them with brooms outstretched. "They'll drive them right outside the yard fence, and they'll go right in."

With the population decline in the area, the need to be self-sufficient is again as necessary as it was one hundred years ago. One of the two standby generators on the ranch is outside the building where the piglets go to stay warm. If the heat lamps shut off, the piglets will die from the cold. There's a backup for everything here.

Keith's son, Mark (Delores's grandson), makes knives, mostly for hunting, on the side. It's another facet of ranch income, but mostly a hobby for now. Mark seems to have inherited a trait on the farm of talented humility. He hones his craft on nights and weekends in his shop when he's not on the ranch driving cattle or breaking horses. The first time I went out to see him, he couldn't get away; he was at a critical point in the corral with a new horse he was training to work with cattle.

This independent spirit and way of life is not entirely lost on the current generation, but it has perhaps taken different forms, partly due to opportunity and partly due to economics. As ranches consolidate, there are fewer families who can even provide the option to return to the family operation. Mark, now twenty-five, went to high school in Valentine and was the only one in his class of sixty-three students to return to the family ranch to work. "A lot of kids, if they had the opportunity, they didn't take it." Mark could be rare in that he considers returning to the ranch an opportunity at all. It's not easy work, like can be found in town, but Mark is suited to it. "It's something different every day here." One day it's pitching hay and tending cattle. The next day Mark will help fix a windmill or a car or help with the pigs his father raises. Another, he'll spend time on his workbench perfecting his hunting knives, entirely handmade from brass, carbon steel, wood and leather. They're well known in the county and, like his father's pigs, are sold entirely by word of mouth. Mark has a business card advertising his handcrafted work knives, but his father, Keith, has no e-mail address, no website or business card. You can find him in the Sand Hills regional phonebook. That has been enough information to keep him in business.

Today, if you want a steak in the Sand Hills, an interesting dichotomy unfolds. If you are fortunate enough to know someone to split up a side of beef at the local meat processor for private use, and if you can store hundreds of pounds of meat, you are able to eat your own steak or one raised and butchered locally. If you don't fall into this category, you will likely stop at your local grocery market, whose beef may or may not be Nebraskan and could have been shipped to a neighboring state to the nearest USDA-approved slaughterhouse, processed and then shipped back to Nebraska to sell at retail. Almost unanimously, people prefer to know the origin and the treatment of their meat before they consume it. As the choice itself dwindles and the food supply chain continues to consolidate and confound, as long as there are still local meat processors who will process meat for private use, there will be quality, traceable meat to eat. Ranches like the Morgan Ranch are proud to say that they can trace their cattle from "gate to plate," a rarity in today's beef industry.

Ranches all over the Sand Hills are making transitions like this to remain competitive and viable today. The Morgan family ranch in Loup County is an original homestead family, with its roots in traditional ranching on their land. Four generations have weathered the ups and downs of the Depression and drought and have pivoted their business into a multigenerational, multinational meat distributing company. In 1992, they introduced Wagyu cattle to their ranch and are still raising this special breed, shipping the meat to a worldwide customer base. When raised in the Kobe province in Japan, these cows become "Kobe beef," some of the most expensive beef in the world. In or out of the Kobe region, Wagyu is known for its richness, consistent marbling and depth of flavor that some would describe as Umami—achieving components of the "fifth" flavor, a deep earthiness that extends beyond salty, sour, spicy and sweet. The Morgans are approved to sell their beef to the European Union, and one of the Morgan sons, Dan, travels to food shows all over the world introducing their meat to new customers abroad.

Restaurant owners and high-end chefs want to know where the food they serve is coming from, so the ranch sets up early summer visits to host their international clientele and sell the beef here in the United States to high-end restaurants all over the country. Dan also travels to California's wine country, Napa Valley, which has also become a gourmet food destination.

It did not always used to be this way, but people have expanded their definition of a meal to include what to drink with it. Wineries have popped up across Nebraska. One in the Sand Hills is George Paul Vinegars, in Cody. George Paul Johnson began experimental plantings of grapevines in 1999 on his land and uses them today to produce small-batch vinegars that are exported to high-end restaurants all over the country. He still makes red and white wines on the premises but today is well known for his line of hand-crafted vinegars. He makes apple cider vinegar, red, white and a balsamic style. Like the Morgans, the Johnsons have found a loyal customer base in high-end restaurants in cities.

The small but mighty renaissance of the homesteading spirit as the next generation searches for its voice is found in a pint glass in Ord. Just on the edge of the Sand Hills is an unlikely entrant into the locally grown market: Scratchtown Brewing Company, opened in October 2013. It's a very small-batch nanobrewery, producing thirty barrels of hyper-local beer each month. Mike Klimek, Jade Stunkel and Caleb Pollard, a native Nebraskan, grow some of the hops they need for brewing batches locally. They see no limits to the opportunities in the Sand Hills and are champions of the region, and they are doing their part to reduce rural "brain drain" as younger generations leave small towns for larger cities in search of work.

"There was this notion that small-town Sandhillers didn't appreciate fine things. When we opened, we hit a nerve in a good way and are completely humbled at the response," Caleb says. Their first-year business goal was to produce 150 barrels of beer. After six months, they hit that. By the end of the year, he anticipates that they will have produced 300 barrels, twice what they anticipated creating.

On the very edge of the Sand Hills, nanobrewery Scratchtown Brewing Company opened in 2013, brewing six styles of beer. It's a welcome new business by the next generation of Sandhillers in the region.

Scratchtown Brewing Company has doubled down on the locally sourced business model. In addition to local hops production, it is also in heavy development with farmers to start planting rye, white wheat and barley—crops absent from the region but necessary for Scratchtown to use to make a truly local product. The brewery makes beer for the "craft beer curious." Caleb is careful to mention that they are not beer snobs, and they see a great opportunity to pair their product with local foods. They work with local meat maker Cetak's Meat Market to create sausage and charcuterie that complement their ales. "Rural revitalization is really important to us. These towns matter, as small as they are. But they have to have compelling stories to contribute to them and give people a reason to come."

Mark Colburn sums it up: "You can do anything you want here." His ancestors and ancestors of families all over the Sand Hills have said this for a century. The region was settled by those who had the exact same determination. For the Colburns, diversification and teamwork means survival, much like it was 150 years ago in the Sand Hills. His father, Keith, just reacquired part of the original Max Wendler place, about 1,500 acres that, for a short time, was sold out of the family. He'll ranch that just like the rest of the land. I asked Delores, "Are you hoping for a sixth generation?" She replied, "We're working on it. We are working on it."

In 2012, there were 49,969 farms listed in the USDA Census of Agriculture, 2,257 more farms than in the 2007 census. This is one of only two upticks in numbers of registered farms in Nebraska since 1935.

AFTERWORD

When I began testing recipes and bringing Sand Hills recipes back to life, I had no idea that they would also bring a few new items into my kitchen. The items below are must-haves for plains kitchen cooking.

Cast-Iron Skillet

A twelve-inch cast-iron skillet with a helper handle (who can lift one with one hand, especially if it's full?) is my most used pan in the kitchen. This is possibly the ultimate prairie kitchen piece of kitchen equipment. Used both on the stovetop and in the oven, cast iron is a fantastic collector and radiator of heat and delivers consistent heat with minimal temperature fluctuation. Because of these virtues, patience is key. Let it preheat slowly over the burner closest in diameter to the skillet; generally speaking, medium-high is the highest heat you'll ever use. Once cast iron is heated, it radiates heat evenly, which was important in earlier frontier days when the stoves were fired with inefficient corncobs or cow chips. Still today, it is a workhorse in the kitchen, yielding evenly browned pancakes, large hash-style dinners and fried chicken. This essential item was once such a staple that it is still found in many hardware stores. Cast iron takes a lot of abuse, and with just a little care up front, it will season into good use for a lifetime.

Can of Bacon Grease

The cans of bacon drippings next to the stove our mothers and grandmothers used to keep have all but disappeared in today's cooking. It was a staple pantry ingredient from the 1920s until roughly the 1970s for almost everyone I spoke to when researching recipes. After cooking with it when re-creating oral recipes, I realized that you're throwing away flavor when you discard it. Yes, it's saturated fat, but when used judiciously, it still adds a deep, rich flavor to dishes. I didn't before, but I now keep a small glass jelly jar of saved drippings in the refrigerator. I try to buy only uncured bacon and discard the grease after a month, starting over at that time. If you store drippings in glass, be sure to let the drippings cool to warm before pouring them in.

DISHPAN

You see them now primarily in antique stores and as garden accessories, but the large, enameled metal dishpans were workhorses in plains kitchens. They were used to make large batches of cookies and breads, as well as in bringing items up from the cellar. Although times have changed, the same dishpan was also used to haul water from the well and was a basin in which to wash dishes and linens. Not only does it accommodate a large recipe, its deep walls also prevent the mess from mixing flour from spreading all over the counter. It makes the batch of dough easy to transport (you can get a hip under a dishpan wall lip). A clean dishpan can be lined with a towel, and the baked rolls, bread or cookies can be sent to the table in it. I found mine at agrisupply.com.

VINTAGE GRINDER

A good manual, adjustable grinder has made its way into my kitchen. Not much about it has changed in one hundred years; there's no electricity required, and it grinds by pulverizing objects between two jagged steel plates rather than pulverizing with spinning blades. Seeing this kitchen item pop up in a number of family histories in my research, I decided to go in search of one. For coffee, I'll never go back to an electric grinder. Some pieces of 150-year-old technology are still around for a reason!

A GOOD KNIFE

The most important tool in your kitchen should be a splurge. One good, sharp, well-cared-for chef's knife will do anything in the kitchen. We've gotten used to choices: serrated knives, short, long, heavy, thin, pressed, forged and even knives designed for a specific task like filleting fish or slicing tomatoes. These are all great to have, but I was surprised how much one really fantastic knife gets used all over the kitchen. On one of my visits to the Colburn ranch, I purchased one of Delores's grandson's. It's by far the sharpest and most beautiful utility knife in my kitchen.

AFTERWORD

New, Fresh Baking Powder
I can't stress enough how important it is to update your leaveners in the pantry every three to six months. What a difference fresh baking soda and powder make in the kitchen! Baking powder was one of the hardest-working ingredients in a Sand Hills pantry, mostly because it was one of the only leaveners available next to eggs. One can of baking powder on the farm was usually used quickly enough that it never had the chance to lose potency.

An Instant-Read Thermometer/Digital Thermometer
This takes the guesswork out of the fried chicken recipe. In today's kitchens, with our ingredients coming from farther and farther away, increasing risk of points of contamination, this is as much a necessity as a cast-iron skillet for these recipes.

Notes from the Author

A note on "Sand Hills" versus "Sandhills": In my research, "Sand Hills" is the spelling used to describe the area as a geographical region. Colloquially, and especially in modern times, it's spelled "Sandhills." For the purposes of this book, I've used the geographical designation of the region as the spelling throughout the book.

A note on recipe testing: For any recipes with flour, I used Dakota Maid unbleached flour. Dakota Maid is based in North Dakota. All flour has been sifted once before measurement.

In Los Angeles, California, one of the most densely populated regions in the nation and where I write and produce various television and online media content, I met and hired a producer, a fellow midwesterner from Ohio. She has all the hallmarks of a good midwestern upbringing, which is mostly why I hired her. She works more slowly to do a task right the first time. She plans out her work and doesn't stop until the work is done. Finally, she is humble about the tenacity of this work ethic. As I introduced her around the office, I said to one of our co-workers, "This is Caitlin, our new producer. She's also from the Midwest, so she's good stock." Our co-worker replied as they shook hands, "Wow, in some environments, that could be a sexist thing to say!" Caitlin said to the woman, "No, where we come from, that's a compliment!"

BIBLIOGRAPHY

Allen, James T. *Creameries and Dairying in Nebraska*. N.p., 1883.
————. *Handbook for Prairie Planting.* 1884.
Bleed, Ann S., and Charles A. Flowerday. *Atlas of the Sand Hills*. Lincoln: University of Nebraska Press, 1998.
Bohemian-American Cook Book. Omaha, NE: Automatic Printing Company, 1949. Collection of author.
Brown, Kevin. *Sandhills Grandmother*. N.p., 1981. Archived at Nebraska State Historical Society, Lincoln, Nebraska.
Brownlee Favorite Recipes. 1876–1976. Private collection.
Bullis, Olive. "Go in and Possess the Land." N.p., n.d. Archived at Cherry County Historical Society, Valentine, Nebraska.
Compendium of Western Nebraska.
Cox, Dan. *Settling the Nebraska Sandhills.* Knutson Enterprises.
Curd, Rollin. *History of Western Boundaries of Nebraska.* N.p.: Boundaries Publishing Company, 1999.
Custer County Cookbook. Compiled by the Home Demonstration Club and Home Extension Council, 1961. Collection of author.
Dick, Everett. *The Sod House Frontier.* Lincoln: University of Nebraska Press, 1937.
Drews, Helen Sawyer. *Shadows Along Pelican Lake.* N.p., n.d. Archived at Cherry County Historical Society, Valentine, Nebraska.
1886 Cattlemen's Association Papers. Collection of Mari Sandoz Heritage Society Library, Chadron, Nebraska.

BIBLIOGRAPHY

Fairmont Creamery Company. *Fairmont Creamery Company History.* N.p., n.d. Archived at Nebraska State Historical Society, Lincoln, Nebraska.

Favorite Recipes. Compiled by the Dodge County Extension Clubs, Nebraska, circa 1960. Collection of author.

Favorite Recipes from the Sandhills. Compiled by the Women's Fellowship of the United Church of Christ, Purdum, Nebraska. Collection of author.

Frontier Stories, Custer County Nebraska. Broken Bow, NE: Custer County Chief, 1936.

Future Homemakers of America. Spring 1979 Cookbook, Garfield or Loup County. Collection of author.

Gilmore, Melvin. *Uses of Plants by the Indians of the Missouri River Region.* Lincoln: University of Nebraska Press, 2014.

Graber, Kay. *Nebraska Pioneer Cookbook.* Lincoln: University of Nebraska Press, 1974.

Holley, Bertie Boyles. "Family Life in a Sandhills Sod House Northwest of Thedford, Nebraska."

Holley, Edna. "Family Life in the Sandhills." Family history, n.d.

Horsman, Reginald. *Feast or Famine.* Columbia: University of Missouri Press, 2008.

Jones, Stephen. *The Last Prairie.* N.p.: International Marine/Ragged Mountain Press, 2000.

Keller, Dorothy. "Family History." N.p., n.d.

Kindscher, Kelly. *Edible Wild Plants of the Prairie.* Lawrence: University Press of Kansas, 1987.

Kramer, Marie. *Grandchildren of the Pioneers.* GoogleBooks. Infinity Publisher.

Kucharka Ceska. Compiled by Past Chief's Association Pythian Sisters, circa 1963. Collection of author.

McIntosh, Charles Barron. *The Nebraska Sand Hills.* Lincoln: University of Nebraska Press, 1996.

Milk Ordinance Laws, Hastings, Nebraska, 1934. Nebraska State Historical Society Archives.

Motl, Erna. *Geographical Interpretation of the Sandhills.*

Mullen Public Schools. *The Mullen Roundup.*

Murray, Rena. "Small Family History."

Nebraska as It Is. 1878.

Newton, Adelaide Rowley. *As the Wind Blows.* Family history.

Novak, Matt. "The Great Depression and the Rise of the Refrigerator." *Pacific Standard*, October 9, 2012. psmag.com.

"Only Yesterday." Family history, n.d.

BIBLIOGRAPHY

The Pantry Shelf. Vol. 2. Burwell, NE: Burwell Tribune Publishing. Collection of author.

Paul, Rodman W. *The Far West and the Great Plains in Transition, 1859–1900.* New York: Harper & Row, 1988.

Powers, William K. *Sacred Foods of the Lakota.* 1990.

Sandhills Thedford-Hyannis Chapter DAR Cookbook. 1991. Private collection.

Smith, Robert. "Who Killed Lard?" NPR—Planet Money, February 3, 2012. npr.org/blogs/money.

Teaford, Mildred Hale. *Bend with the Wind.* Kearney, NE: Morris Publications, 2004.

Thornburg, Billie Lee Snyder. *Bertie and Me,* 2003.

Wishart, David. *The Last Days of the Rainbelt.* Lincoln: University of Nebraska Press, 2013.

Yost, Nellie Snyder. *Call of the Range.* Athens: Ohio University Press, 1966.

ARCHIVES

Cherry County Historical Society Archives, Valentine, Nebraska.

Custer County Historical Society Archives, Broken Bow, Nebraska.

Garfield County Historical Society Archives, Burwell, Nebraska.

Mari Sandoz Center Library Archives, Chadron, Nebraska.

Nebraska State Historical Society, General Archives, Lincoln, Nebraska.

Nebraska State Historical Society, Union Pacific Manuscripts, Lincoln, Nebraska.

Union Pacific Railroad Company Archives, Council Bluffs, Iowa.

INDEX

INDEX

ABOUT THE AUTHOR

Christianna Reinhardt spent her early childhood in Loup County, Nebraska. A writer and television producer, she has written for *Saveur, Specialty Food* magazine, *Omaha World-Herald, Inspired Living Omaha,* Yahoo! Shine, Blackboardeats.com and blogs at BurwellGeneralStore. com. The Emmy-nominated television producer has worked with top culinary talent Tyler Florence, Giada De Laurentiis, Guy Fieri and Aida Mollenkamp and writes and directs television and online lifestyle content for Food Network, Cooking Channel, Travel Channel and Yahoo! In 2005, she purchased the Carnegie Library in Burwell, Nebraska, and converted it into a residence. She splits her time between Burwell and Venice, California. This is her first book.

Courtesy of Benjamin Busch.

Please visit BurwellGeneralStore.com to find additional recipes, photos and stories discovered in the Sand Hills and find Christianna on Twitter @ BurwellGeneral.